How **PERFECT** *is your* **PARTNER?**

Phillip Hodson is a psychotherapist, sex therapist, and marriage counselor. In addition to his private practice, he teaches and lectures regularly, and is Chief Spokesperson for the British Association for Counselling and Psychotherapy. He has written eleven books, and contributed columns for several newspapers and magazines and appears regularly on television.

PENGUIN
COMPASS

How PERFECT is your PARTNER?

50 WAYS TO GET TO KNOW YOUR LOVER

PHILLIP HODSON

with the assistance of Joel Levy

PENGUIN COMPASS

PENGUIN BOOKS

Published by the Penguin Group
Penguin Group (USA) Inc., 375 Hudson Street, New York, New York
10014, U.S.A
Penguin Group (Canada), 10 Alcorn Avenue, Toronto, Ontario, Canada
M4V 3B2 (a division of Pearson Penguin Canada Inc.)
Penguin Books Ltd, 80 Strand, London WC2R 0RL, England
Penguin Ireland, 25 St Stephen's Green, Dublin 2, Ireland (a division of
Penguin Books Ltd)
Penguin Group (Australia), 250 Camberwell Road, Camberwell, Victoria
3124, Australia (a division of Pearson Australia Group Pty Ltd)
Penguin Books India Pvt Ltd, 11 Community Centre, Panchsheel Park,
New Delhi - 110 017, India
Penguin Group (NZ), cnr Airborne and Rosedale Roads, Albany,
Auckland, New Zealand (a division of Pearson New Zealand Ltd)
Penguin Books (South Africa) (Pty) Ltd, 24 Sturdee Avenue, Rosebank,
Johannesburg 2196, South Africa

Penguin Books Ltd, Registered Offices:
80 Strand, London WC2R 0RL, England

First published in Great Britain by Carroll & Brown Publishers Limited
2004
Published in Penguin Books 2005

1 3 5 7 10 9 8 6 4 2

Text copyright © Phillip Hodson, 2004
Illustrations and compilation © Carroll & Brown Limited 2004
All rights reserved

CIP data available
ISBN 0-14-219636-3

Reproduced by RALI, Spain
Printed and bound in China by SNP
Set in Perpetua and GillSans
Art Editors Peggy Sadler and Anne Fisher

 Are You Physically Compatible?

 Are You Sexually Compatible?

CONTENTS

Foreword

It's long been known that professional matchmakers are more successful at picking couples for lasting partnerships than if matters are left to fate. Research carried out as early as the 1970s shows that matrimonial agencies, by pinpointing areas of compatibility, are highly skilled at pairing people off. Should we therefore abandon our western romantic ideals and sign up with the nearest bureau of arranged marriages? Well, matchmakers may be efficient but human beings have an inconvenient tendency to fall in lust. By the time you get around to considering the safeguards offered by personality testing, you feel crazy about the individual standing by your side (and I mean "crazy"). Blind with erotic desire, the last thing on your mind is common sense and analyzing your genuine compatibilities.

This book is therefore exceptionally valuable for newer couples because it allows you to take a reality check even while you are at the "lustful" stage. If you're already feeling swept away, you can do a backwards check. Or if you are already in a long-term partnership, you can use it to assess areas of strength and highlight areas of relating that may need more attention.

Most long-term couples have the same broad approaches to life or share complementary values. However, even for those with significant personal differences, this book will be an essential aid. Conflicts always occur in relationships, but the successful formula for a long-term relationship takes into account how you manage your problems. This book will help you assess your compatibility with 50 proven tests, and give you sensible suggestions about ways to overcome the differences.

How Perfect Is Your Partner? also takes into account the fact that there are major changes today in the way men and women approach long-term commitment. First of all, most of us, regardless of whether we actually marry, take the birth of our children as the really permanent commitment to the future. And statistics show that today's couples think long and hard before embarking on the joys and perils of parenthood. Secondly, more people than ever are remaining single these days. Around one in six households are of single people. It is even predicted that 30 per cent of women will remain childless through choice.

I don't take this to mean that we have lost confidence in long-term relationships, just that these are difficult to manage in the new climate where women share equal power with men. On the contrary, I think we all long for a soulmate but our standards have been raised. If you ask young men and women what they want out of life, they still universally declare that they long "to love and be loved." That great need does not go away.

The author of this book, Phillip Hodson, a psychotherapist and sex therapist, has spent a working lifetime helping lovers enjoy their loving, long-term relationships and family life. As a popular TV and radio counselor, he has, in this book, transformed his counseling skills into a series of fascinating tests. Through his provocative questions and suggestions you can discover your strengths and weaknesses, both as individuals and as a couple. You can also get to know yourself better, *and* have a lot of fun doing so. Fun tends to get left out of the marital equation yet fun is one of the main elements that appeals when the two of you first get to know each other.

Phillip's methods have definitely worked for me. I should come clean here and declare that I myself have been in a long-term relationship for thirty years, which has included storms as well as sunshine. The man I love has taught me a great deal during this time but I hope and presume that he has learned something from me too. When you hear that the man in my life is the author of this book, you will understand why I find his methods so persuasive. Many of the methods and ideas between these covers have helped us to survive into our current age and stage of love, affection, and continuing compatibility. The proof of the pudding is in the eating.

Anne Hooper

Introduction

The main theme of this book is that people with similar temperaments and personalities get along best. It is the Rule of Similarity. Contrary to popular folk wisdom, opposites *never* attract as strongly. Even when polar opposites marry, they rarely achieve harmony. They are far more likely to end up in the divorce courts than to grow old together sitting on the porch rocker.

The more similar you are to your partner the more compatible you are and the better your chances of long-term relationship success. This rule applies even at the most basic level of physical characteristics such as finger length, right up to your more complicated social and cultural attributes.

Over 90 per cent of the married couples in major Western countries are from the same race and mostly of the same religion, education, sociological class, intelligence, and even share physical characteristics like body shape. Even couples who date regularly typically share the same political values, views on sex, and sexual roles. Couples who are the most similar at the beginning of their relationship are also the ones most likely to stay together in the long run. Married couples who experience the least marital conflict are those with similar personalities. They usually even enjoy the same TV programs. When we look for a life partner, it seems, we are seeking a double.

Complementarity vs similarity

The only contradicting evidence to this general principle involves our reproductive cells. Here, nature requires us to avoid mating with those who are over-similar genetically. If we all married our siblings, like the rulers of ancient Egypt, there would be a greater risk of inbreeding. We can call this principle the Rule of Complementarity – the opposite to the Rule of Similarity. How can we explain the apparent contradiction between the rule of similarity and the rule of complementarity? The latter rule seems to apply only at a basic, genetic level, while the former applies to the meaningful things like aspirations, ideals, and whether you both like the *Simpsons*. Perhaps the explanation is to be found in the field of evolutionary psychology, a branch of science that looks at why humans have evolved with their characteristic behaviors.

Evolutionary psychology suggests that when you are procreating, it is the quality of the genetic contribution that a partner can provide to any offspring that is most important. This is one area where the rule of complementarity applies (as we'll see in Part 1, in some crucial areas parents need to be genetically dissimilar to improve the likely genetic quality of their offspring) and may account for the short duration of many marriages although there are children.

By contrast, different rules apply when you're looking for a long-term life partner. In this situation you don't care about the amino-acid code of specific genes, but about whether you will still be able to love one another in twenty years. Here, the rule of similarity applies. To summarize briefly: complementarity is important when it comes to getting it on; similarity when it comes to getting along. That is why it's possible to like strangers with whom you have nothing else in common than the desire to go to bed, and why sex in a long-term relationship may not be entirely rapturous.

Emotional love

When we fall head over heels in love with someone we start to use very revealing language. We say things like "It's as if I have known you all my life"... "You are like my other half"... "I know what you are going to say before you say it"... "You remind me of me." Because you are too young to know any better, the first people you tend to fall in love with are your parents. The qualities you will therefore admire in others are based on family traits and traditions. I don't mean you have to be attracted to dark-eyed brunettes just because these were the facial characteristics of your opposite sexed parent. I mean the "type" of person who attracts you will probably have some sort of look that reminds your brain of the people from whom you originated. For most of your life, you have probably been looking, albeit unconsciously, for a person who does remind you of you, as this book proves.

How to use this book

How Perfect Is Your Partner? is organized into physical, sexual, psychological, economic and social, and psychic compatibility sections, and contains a final section on how to put it all together to come up with the overall harmony rating for you and your partner. At the end, you will also find my plan for an ideal (or idealized) partnership under the somewhat misleading title of "perfect partnership," but I am well aware of the fact that nothing in human life is perfect.

You can work through the tests one after another, dip in and out as you wish, or choose an order based on the issues that interest you most, but it's very important

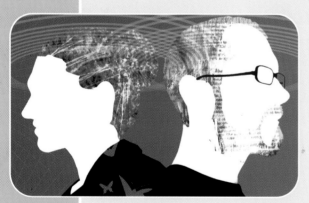

to take these tests simply as a guide. The tests have not been tested on a significantly large sample to find what the average score is for a population, however this doesn't matter in nearly all cases because we're using the tests for comparison. In other words, what's important is not how you score in relation to an "average" population, but how you score in relation to your partner.

This book contains tests that are both significant and fun, and while the text for each test gives you an idea of how seriously you should take your result, in the event that the results for you and your partner do not match for a given test, the final section of the book goes a step further and provides a handy tool to help you interpret the general significance of your findings.

I must stress when you work out your Overall Compatibility Rating (see page 146) this is not intended to trigger a separation or divorce, but instead should start a dialogue between you and your partner. A book like this can only be a starting point for exploring your relationship. Every relationship is unique and poses unique questions that can only be properly answered by you and your partner, possibly with a little guidance from professionals. A therapist of some sort (and they can take many forms, from friends or parents to priests or psychiatrists) can give advice and insight tailored to your specific case in a way that a book cannot quite achieve.

Good news about emotional convergence

But if you and your partner are lucky enough to share similar personalities and interests, the good news is that things may only get better. After the initial honeymoon effect has worn off, and sexual frequency slows from daily to every few days or so, a new relationship reinforcer tends to come into play.

Psychologists at Northwestern University have identified a phenomenon called "emotional convergence." This shows that over time partners begin to view major life events through similar spectacles. They have the same or similar reactions to major ups and downs. They even finish each other's sentences. Small inhibitions disappear. Women who previously never laughed out loud, for example, learn to do so. While one person is strongly sympathetic to a cause, the other increasingly respects it. The effect also applies to bad behavior, unfortunately. Research coordinator Dr Cameron Anderson cites the case of film star Elizabeth Taylor who learned to drink and swear to excess from her alcoholic husband Richard Burton. He says that overall it is surprising just how much people do change their emotions and inhibitions as a result of a relationship. Perhaps this research helps us demonstrate the truth behind our western romantic ideal: given long enough, and given enough love, two people do tend to become one.

PHILLIP HODSON

PART ONE

Are You Physically Compatible?

The most obvious factor in determining physical compatibility is the one that came into play the first time you and your partner saw each other – physical attractiveness. The fact that you found each other attractive enough to strike up a relationship indicates a fairly high level of physical compatibility. The tests in this section look at some of the elements that may have been involved, although you did not realize it, in this immediate physical attraction, together with other elements whose effects will only become apparent in the long-term.

Physical similarity

As we saw in the introduction, the essential ingredient in long-term compatibility in most couples is similarity. What may surprise you is that this even extends to physical compatibility. Most of us probably dislike the idea that we choose partners because they are physically similar to us, but physical similarity isn't just skin deep and it doesn't simply mean that you are drawn to someone who looks like you.

The sort of physical traits where similarity does turn out to be important run the gamut from the obvious – things like height and weight – to the unexpected – such as finger length. They even include invisible traits: research has shown that couples have similar levels of nitrogen in their blood, for example. Physical traits are more or less controlled by your genes, and this sort of research has convinced many scientists that people are somehow attracted to others who have similar genes to them. In fact, the apparent imperative to unconsciously seek genetic similarity could be the underlying reason that similarity is the rule in compatibility.

Why do people with similar genes attract?

As far as nature is concerned, the point of being with someone is for you to have kids and make sure your genes get passed on to the next generation, and what better way to do this than to pair up with someone who has similar ones to you? Incest taboos stop us from taking this logic too far, but outside of your family you're likely to find yourself most attracted to people with similar genes to you. Genetic similarities manifest themselves in very interesting ways – as you'll learn later in this chapter, even the length of your middle finger is an important determinant. This isn't always the case, however. As we'll see in the Smelly T-shirt Test, sometimes having complementary genes is an important factor in genetic compatibility.

The rules of attraction

Slightly more concrete concerns than genetic similarity also play a part in what makes someone attractive. Back in the days of prehistory, evolutionary biologists argue, the qualities that were important in a mate were survival skills and fertility (collectively called "fitness"), and our conscious and unconscious rules of attraction would have evolved to make us good at spotting these qualities. We would have looked for the subtle cues that signaled that potential mates were strong, clever, resourceful, disease-free, good providers, and likely to survive childbirth and raise children well. In fact, the theory goes, we still do, and it is these subtle cues that make someone attractive or not. The tests focusing on beauty, symmetry, and age examine how you and your partner match up when it comes to these cues.

The other tests in this section look at different aspects of physical compatibility, such as unconsciously held templates that we use to select mates, and the purely practical issue of whether your sleeping styles match up.

Eye of the beholder

Ultimately, however, we shouldn't get carried away with the significance of many of these physical compatibility issues. For starters, many of these factors are more essential in the early stages of attraction, and you're obviously already attracted to your partner or you wouldn't be reading this book! Secondly, while in your evolutionary past good genes or markers of fitness may have been important, what matters more now is long-term compatibility, which we'll explore in the later sections.

Do Your Middle Fingers Match?

Contrary to popular folk wisdom, opposites do *not* attract as much as "similars." The more similar you are to your partner, the more compatible you are and the better your chances of long-term relationship success.

Anthropologists have discovered that couples tend to have external, physical similarities. Strangely, the physical feature that is most similar in couples is middle finger length. Finger length also can indicate hormone levels – another correlating factor. Why is this the case? It's all to do with genetics. The length of your middle finger is largely determined by your genes, although other factors such as childhood diet also play a part. Scientists have concluded that people are somehow attracted to others who have similar genes to themselves, including the genes that govern middle finger length. One consequence of this is that a couple is likely to find that their finger lengths match up. In other words, your middle fingers don't bring you together directly, but they do act as a marker of genetic similarity.

The relative lengths of your index and ring fingers (the digits known as 2D and 4D) are partly determined by the

Test 1: Middle Finger Length

Simply determine whether your finger is longer or shorter than average, and how your relative length compares with your partner's.

- Measure the length of the middle finger on your right hand, from where it joins your palm to the tip, and make the same measurement for your partner.
- Compare your scores to the average for your gender.

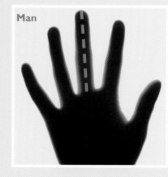

Man

The average length of the middle finger in men is 9.3 centimeters.

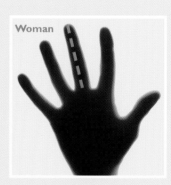

Woman

The average length of the middle finger in women is 8 centimeters.

INTERPRETING THE RESULTS

Match You both have average length middle fingers (give or take 2 millimeters); you both have longer than average middle fingers; or you both have shorter than average middle fingers.

Mismatch If your fingers are wildly disparate, something as simple as childhood diet may be to blame. Many people who have genes for long middle fingers end up with short digits, and vice versa, because of some quirk in development.

WHAT TO DO ABOUT A MISMATCH

A finger-length mismatch isn't a disaster, but it may signal differences in your relationship. You can't change your genes, but you can use your test results as a basis for discussion. Talk about your differences, or try making a list of what you love about your partner, along with a list of the aspects of your relationship you find the most challenging. Positive lists can help you to overcome entrenched negative views of your partner.

levels of sex hormones that your body produces. Men who produce lots of testosterone generally have longer ring fingers relative to their index fingers, and consequently a low 2D:4D ratio. Women who produce high levels of female sex hormones, such as estrogen, prolactin, and luteinizing hormone, generally have shorter ring fingers relative to their index fingers, and consequently a high 2D:4D ratio.

INTERPRETING THE RESULTS

RIGHT HAND 2D: 4D RATIO

	Men	Women
High	0.959 or more	0.976 or more
Average	0.953 – 0.958	0.968 – 0.975
Low	0.952 or less	0.967 or less

Test 2: Index and Ring Finger Length Ratios

- Lay your right hand flat on the table and measure the length, in centimeters, of your index and ring fingers from the "tip" to where they join the palm.
- Divide the figure you get for your index finger by the one you get for your ring finger. For example, if your index finger is 8 cm long and your ring finger is 9 cm long, your 2D: 4D ratio is 8/9, or 0.889.
- To see if your ratio is high, average, or low, compare your result to the chart (right).

In general, men with a low 2D:4D ratio and higher testosterone levels are more compatible with women with a high 2D:4D ratio and high estrogen levels and vice versa. So, two people from opposite categories are more likely to be compatible (equally, if you both fall into the average category you are likely to be more compatible).

Your 2D: 4D ratio can tell you important things about yourself and the qualities that might make a partner more compatible. For example, a man with high testosterone levels is likely to be more aggressive and dominant and more attracted to feminine women who complement these characteristics. But there is an obverse to this: such a man may prefer women who match his aggression and drive.

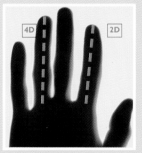

Low ratio
ring finger longer than index finger

High ratio
index finger longer than ring finger

Beauty is obviously a major factor in determining how attractive someone is. Psychologists have even discovered that beautiful people benefit from something called "the halo effect," where they are judged to be more intelligent, competent, charming, and agreeable than less attractive people, purely on the basis of their looks. Evolutionary biologists have found that, in general, the elements that constitute male and female beauty are either those that indicate high levels of exposure to respective sex hormones, such as strong chins and jaw lines in men, or wide hips and a narrow waist in women, or those that indicate good resistance to disease, such as even, regular features (see The Symmetry Test, page 20).

A LEAGUE OF YOUR OWN

But although beauty may make someone more attractive, it doesn't necessarily make them more desirable as a compatible mate. This counter-intuitive finding has been replicated in several different research studies, which suggest that the partners we favor most are those we rate as having a similar standard of beauty to ourselves. So it turns out that your perception of your own looks is what determines the looks you go for in a partner. In other words, the attractive powers of beauty are relatively determined and not absolute.

Someone with low self-perception – i.e. who does not rate him/herself highly on a scale of attractiveness – who pair ups with someone he/she rates as highly attractive is more likely to feel unhappy with the relationship in the long-term than the same person paired with someone he/she rates as equally attractive.

The rating you give yourself is not necessarily the same rating that you would be given by an independent panel of judges. It reflects your self-esteem. The consequence is that people with high self-esteem will feel more comfortable with more beautiful partners, answering the age-old question "how did he/she get a girl/guy like that?"

The Test

Below are beauty rating scales (10 being very beautiful and 1 being positively ugly) for you and your partner. Use the appropriate one honestly to rate yourself, and the other honestly to rate your partner. Then compare the ratings. It may be diplomatic not to let your partner know how you scored this test.

You

10	9	8	7	6	5	4	3	2	1

Your partner

10	9	8	7	6	5	4	3	2	1

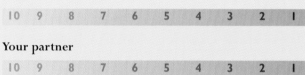

INTERPRETING THE SCORES

Ratings within three points of each other count as a good match. Ratings that are 4 or more points apart count as a mismatch.

WHAT TO DO ABOUT A MISMATCH

You scored higher than your partner The fact that you rated your partner significantly lower than yourself in the looks department suggests that you might be a little dissatisfied with your choice. Focus on the qualities that first attracted you to your partner, which may be less obvious than beauty but no less tangible. How well you are able to do this depends on the extent to which you are swayed by conventional social values and judgments (see Are You Open to New Experiences, page 56).

You scored lower than your partner This is only a problem if you feel that the mismatch makes you uncomfortable. Some people are quite happy to class themselves as less physically attractive than their partner because they have the confidence that their other virtues more than make up for it. If, however, the mismatch is an issue for you, bear in mind that, as I discussed in the background to this test, self-perception does not necessarily have much to do with objective judgements of beauty or attractiveness. Work on boosting your self-esteem with exercises such as visualizing positive scenarios, making affirmations (e.g. telling yourself "I am a beautiful person") and learning to give yourself proper credit for achievements.

The Symmetry Test

In seeking to understand what constitutes a beautiful face, psychologists have looked in minute detail at faces and features that are judged "beautiful" by panels of observers, and at the faces of models and actors famous for their good looks. Among the most significant of their findings is the revelation that bilateral symmetry is a major component of beauty. Faces that are symmetrical about a line drawn vertically down the middle are judged high on measures of beauty, and the faces of models and actors universally judged to be beautiful display exactly this bilateral symmetry.

What's more, this finding doesn't just apply to humans. Other animals show the same preference for symmetry. For instance, birds seem to find mates with symmetrical tail feathers more attractive than those without. If you cut a few chunks out of an "attractive" bird's tail he will suddenly cease to be such a heartthrob.

Why is bilateral symmetry attractive to us? Why should we have evolved to find it beautiful? The answer seems to be that it correlates with "developmental competence" – genetic and physiological quality or, in layman's terms, good genes and health.

During development, a number of factors can interfere with the steady growth of each side of your body to cause what is known as fluctuating asymmetry. Disease, injury, harmful mutations, poor nutrition – these can all prevent you from growing up symmetrical and lead to one side of your body looking different from the other. So bilateral symmetry functions as a marker for good genes, a good immune system, resistance to disease, the physical prowess to avoid injury, etc. Does your partner's face reveal a high or low degree of developmental competence? This test will help you decide.

The Test

Normally photographs of faces are computer processed to get an accurate measure of symmetry, but here you're going to use a much less technical approach to make an entirely subjective judgment of the bilateral symmetry of your partner's face.

1 Find a large (10 x 8 inch, if possible), full-face photograph of your partner.

2 Take a piece of tracing paper the same size as the photograph, and mark out a grid of 80 squares.

3 Lay the paper over the photo and make an exact trace of your partner's face including the jawline and main features (eyes, nose, mouth, eyebrows, ears, hairline) to get a line drawing. The grid should make it easier to trace the features.

4 Fold the drawing down the center line and cut it in half along this line.

5 Take the left-hand half and turn it over, then use another sheet of tracing paper, cut to the same size, to trace over it.

6 Turn the original half-trace back over and fit the two together. Repeat the procedure for the right-hand half of the face. Now you have two pictures that show two versions of what your partner would look like if his/her face was exactly symmetrical. Now compare the artificially symmetrical versions with each other and with the real photo. How similar are they to one another? Would you categorize them as very similar, not very similar, or totally dissimilar?

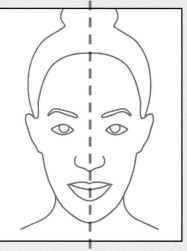

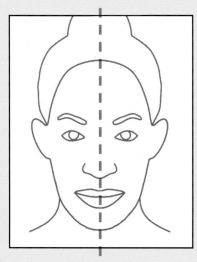

WHAT TO DO ABOUT A MISMATCH

As you've probably realized, this test is not very scientific, so the results should be taken with a pinch of salt. It can be a shock to see your partner's face recognizable but distorted, but comfort yourself with the thought that while our Stone-Age ancestors might have needed to use developmental competence as a valid criterion for mate selection, in today's world we value psychological factors like personality and character much more highly. After all, the most symmetrical face in the world doesn't make someone a nice guy or gal.

The Smelly T-shirt Test

One of the most fascinating findings to emerge from the work being done by evolutionary biologists and geneticists is that you might be able to find your most genetically compatible partner by smell. There is strong evidence that your nose can pick up incredibly subtle but definite olfactory cues that tell you whether someone has the right genes to be your perfect partner, especially if you are female. A recent study found that, particularly for females, how someone smells is the single most important variable in choosing a lover.

GENETIC COMPATIBILITY

The genes involved in this phenomenon are a group common to many animals, collectively known as the major histo-compatibility complex (MHC), although in humans the MHC is also known as the human leukocyte antigen system (HLA for short). HLA genes are found on chromosome 6 and play a vital role in the immune system.

In evolutionary terms, the best person to mate with is the person with whom you can have the "best" children (best here being most resistant to disease). That person will be the person who has the most different HLA genes from you, so that when your genes combine with theirs to produce offspring, the new combination is as novel as possible. This means that HLA genetics is one of the few areas where you and your partner are more compatible the less similar you are.

Research on how people pair off has shown that they do indeed seem to prefer mates who have different HLA genes than their own. But how do they know? The day when you can check a potential partner's genetic sequence directly still exists only in science fiction, so people must be giving off some subtle physical message that somehow communicates signals about their genes. Studies with mice, for which scent is a particularly important means of communication, suggested that smell might be the answer.

THE T-SHIRT EXPERIMENT

To see if smell was the signaling mechanism in humans as well as mice, a team at the University of Bern devised a simple test using smelly T-shirts, on which this test is

The Test

To recreate the smelly T-shirt test for yourself you will need some male volunteers. For the test to work properly the female partner needs to be in the dark about whose T-shirt is whose, so you should try and get a third party to act as coordinator, or failing that the male partner should be the coordinator (although ideally he too should be unaware of what is going on to avoid giving the game away). It's also necessary for the female partner not to be taking contraceptive pills. Ideally, the test should be timed to coincide with when she's ovulating.

1 Wash as many identical T-shirts as there are men (you need at least four men in total, or the odds of choosing your partner by chance alone are just too high – 44 men took part in the Swiss experiment).

2 Each man, including the male partner, should wear one of the T-shirts for two consecutive nights, before sealing it, unwashed, into a clean plastic bag. Label the bag with the identity of the wearer, but this should be known only to the coordinator.

3 Put each T-shirt into a separate, numbered, odor-free cardboard box, with a hole cut in the top to allow sniffing. Make sure that a record is kept of whose T-shirt is in which box.

4 Get the female partner to sniff each box in turn. She should rate each T-shirt from 0–10 on its "sexiness" and "pleasantness" level (10 being the most appealing). The coordinator records these ratings, totalling them to give an overall rating for each T-shirt.

5 The coordinator should now reveal the rating assigned to each T-shirt. The better the T-shirt rating, the more compatible you are with its wearer.

based. Their findings revealed that women preferred the T-shirts of men whose HLA genes were most different from their own. These also turned out to be the T-shirts they said smelled most like their partners, suggesting that they really were using this method to select partners. Crucially, the women in the experiment were not taking birth control pills and were ovulating (i.e. at their most fertile) when the experiment was done.

What was it those women were smelling? The answer is probably pheromones – mysterious but powerful scent molecules that have been compared to hormones that travel outside the body. Like hormones, these chemicals can trigger reactions throughout the body, even in the mind. In this case, pheromones given off by the sweat glands of the men triggered the women's sexual and emotional responses. No one is exactly sure how pheromones work, but it seems clear that they can somehow communicate information about the genetic makeup of the person giving them off.

WHAT TO DO ABOUT A MISMATCH

Depending on whose T-shirt got the highest rating, this test could lead to some embarrassment. But don't worry, because there are several points to consider:

• The original experiment showed a *correlation* between women's preferences and HLA variability, not an *exact matching* between women and their partners. If you took 100 couples and arranged them according to smelly T-shirt ratings, you would find that most women would end up near their partners; very few would end up actually opposite; and some would be nowhere near. A correlation is not the same as an exact causal link.

• Because you're only using one T-shirt smell-tester, and probably not very many men, your version of the test is a long way from being statistically significant.

• HLA variability has no bearing on the future of your relationship – it won't mean you have fewer arguments, better sex, or greater marital satisfaction.

Although your psychology may seem to be independent from your physiology, many aspects of the latter can greatly affect your personality attributes, hobbies and pastimes, likes and dislikes, and other practical aspects of your everyday life. This test looks at issues surrounding your energy levels, and how they match up with your partner's, but energy levels are just one aspect of the metabolic and physiological processes of your body. Other issues you need to consider include how well you metabolize certain types of food and whether there are classes of food that are off-limits to you, which could make your eating habits incompatible with your partner's. Another issue is whether and how well you can tolerate alcohol. People from some ethnic backgrounds have a high chance of lacking the gene for the enzyme that metabolizes alcohol, making them unable to tolerate alcohol at all – which could be a big issue if your partner likes to party and you can't drink a drop.

Your energy levels affect your life in many ways. For instance, if one partner is full of beans at the end of the day while the other is fatigued and dopey, they will irritate or disappoint one another. Similar scenarios could affect how well you and your partner share hobbies, agree on where to eat, or get along while on vacation. This test seeks to assess your energy levels by looking at factors that contribute to them, including your metabolism, lifestyle, and diet, and visible signs of them, including attention span, fatigue levels, and fitness.

The Questionnaire

You and your partner should both complete this quiz and then compare results.

1 **Some people can eat all day and not gain an ounce. What's the relationship between your food intake and your weight?**
a   *I burn through chocolate like a hot knife through butter and never gain weight.*
b   *If I stick to healthy foods the pounds won't stick to me.*
c   *I only have to look at a cookie to gain 20 pounds.*

2 **Which of the following best describes your normal daily diet?**
a   *Low carbs, low fat, high fiber.*
b   *Meat and potatoes.*
c   *Junk food.*

3 **How do you feel when you get up in the morning?**
a   *Fit and full of energy.*
b   *Initially woosy but soon up to speed.*
c   *Like the living dead.*

4 **How do you usually feel at the end of the day?**
a   *Sparky and bright.*
b   *A bit tired.*
c   *Out on my feet.*

5 **What sort of attention span do you have?**
a   *A gnat's (short).*
b   *A dog's (medium).*
c   *A sloth's (patient and long).*

6 **What effect does caffeine have on your system?**
a   *One cup of coffee and I'm wired.*
b   *A cup of coffee perks me up a little.*
c   *I need ten gallons of coffee just to get on my feet in the morning.*

7 **When you're on a summer vacation what sort of activities do you favor?**
a   *Hiking, water sports, tennis — anything that keeps me active.*
b   *A bit of sightseeing, walking or sports — interspersed with relaxing by the pool or on the beach.*
c   *Lying blissfully on my back and moving as few muscles as possible.*

INTERPRETING THE RESULTS

How did you score?

Mostly (a)s Hyper (hares)

Mostly (b)s Ordinary (cats)

Mostly (c)s Sedated (tortoises)

If you both got the same category you obviously match up for energy levels, which is good news for your compatibility. You can share dishes at a restaurant, plan holiday activities (or lack of them) together, and agree to stay in and watch TV or to go out and party. If you differed by only one category (intermediate match), then there may be some disagreements in store in the future, while if one of you is Hyper and the other Sedated, your relationship is definitely a mismatch.

WHAT TO DO ABOUT A MISMATCH

There may be occasions when you have to accept that the two of you will have to do separate things, but a couple shouldn't expect to share every activity. What's important to remember is that your partner's desire to leave you on the beach while he/she runs off to climb the nearest mountain, or remains curled up on the sofa when you want to go out dancing, is not a reflection on you or a sign of dislike or abandonment, but simply an expression of your differing metabolic drives.

Many people are consciously aware that they go for a certain type, and there is evidence that, even when we are not aware if it, we tend to follow certain ingrained patterns when it comes to relationships. Several factors contribute to this, including, for instance, agreeableness (see page 58), emotional intelligence (see page 66), and arguing style (see page 90).

A significant factor is that most of us have a template of an ideal partner stored in our unconscious minds – an image against which potential partners are checked and rated. This template includes what our ideal partner looks like, at least in general terms.

WHERE DOES THE TEMPLATE COME FROM?

The ideal partner template derives from many different sources and influences. Cultural and social programming make major contributions through the images and ideals to which you are exposed from childhood onward. As the major influences and role models of our early lives, parents inevitably have an impact. Your opposite sex parent provides a physical, behavioral, and emotional model for your developing concept of the opposite sex. As a child you absorbed and internalized this model. As you got older, more influences fed into your template: teachers and other authority figures; boys or girls at school; figures in the media and popular culture. In this test we'll be looking at the physical aspect of this template – facial profiles.

The Test

How well does your partner match up to your template? To find out, we first need to discover what your template looks like. On the right is a series of photographs of the elements that go together to make a profile. Your task is to pick from them to create a sort of identikit profile, which can then be compared to your partner's profile.

1 For the first profile element, select the one that most appeals to you.

2 With some tracing paper, trace over the photograph of that element.

3 Move onto the second element. Use the alignment marks to help you trace the second element so that it joins up properly with the first.

4 Repeat this process until you have traced an entire identikit profile.

5 As with the Symmetry Test (see page 20), you will now need to make a subjective comparison of the ideal with the actual. Find a side-on photo of your partner and compare the profiles. Are they almost identical, in the same ballpark, moderately different, or worlds apart?

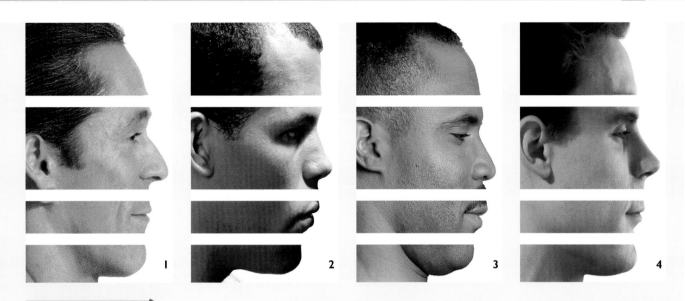

1   2   3   4

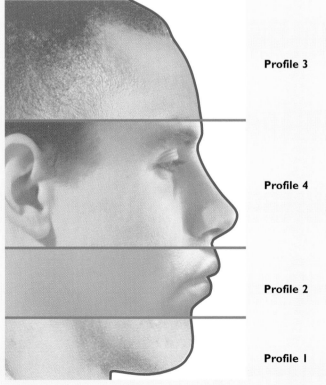

Profile 3

Profile 4

Profile 2

Profile 1

WHAT TO DO ABOUT A MISMATCH

The internalized templates that develop from childhood are not necessarily good things. Many people find themselves repeating unsuccessful or hurtful relationship patterns because of the maladaptive templates they've ended up with. So the profile that lurks within your subconscious does not necessarily represent an ideal in the objective sense.

Also, your partner may conform to your ideal template in other, non-physical ways. Truly compatible partners can look beyond the physical to find the genuine core of their mutual attraction in shared attitudes, experiences, goals, and drives.

What's Your Real Age?

In the past it was perhaps more common than it is today for a husband to be significantly older than his wife and the idea of a man being older than his partner is still unlikely to raise an eyebrow, while the opposite situation is still regarded with some suspicion and disapproval in most societies. Today, most couples are very close in age, with a gap of no more than four or five years between them.

Sharing a similar age is probably a boost to compatibility, implying as it does a higher likelihood of shared interests, priorities and life schedules, and common background of popular culture. So the most straightforward form of age test is to simply compare your ages. The bigger the difference, the more serious the potential consequences for your social, cultural, and psychological compatibility.

BIOLOGICAL VS CHRONOLOGICAL AGE

But what about your physical compatibility? When assessing a prospective partner you need to know his or her age for a variety of straightforward physical reasons: health, fitness, fertility, and life expectancy. But it's not simply the number of years on the clock that count. What you need to assess is your partner's *biological* age as opposed to chronological age; it's the difference between your age in terms of fitness, physiology, and health, and your actual age as measured in years. Poor health habits accelerate biological aging ahead of chronological age, so that you are more likely to suffer ill health and die early for your age. Good health habits, on the other hand, can slow down your biological aging so that, biologically speaking, you have the body of a much younger person.

The Test

Here is a checklist of some of the factors affecting biological aging, positively or negatively. See which factors apply to your partner and add up his/her score.

Biological Aging Factor	Score	Biological Aging Factor	Score
Regular exposure to strong sunlight	5	Living in urban area	4
Smoking (heavy-moderate)	8	Living in countryside	2
Smoking (occasional)	4	Regular exercise	-5
Diet high in processed/refined foods (e.g. junk food)	5	Occupational exposure to pollutants/toxins	5
Diet high in fresh fruit and vegetables	-5	Family history of degenerative disease (atherosclerosis/cancer etc)	4
Late nights	4	High stress levels	2
Heavy drinking	5	Relaxation skills (e.g. meditation, yoga)	-1
Moderate drinking	2	Good hygiene habits (bathing, handwashing, teeth brushing, flossing etc.)	-1
Drug use	5		

Intrinsic factors such as the quality of the DNA repair machinery inside your cells or the health of your chromosomes can cause biological aging. So can "external" factors – mainly sunlight and pollution (including toxins that you take in with food, water, or smoke). The key culprits here are free radicals: highly reactive molecules created by the action of ultraviolet light (in sunlight) or the reactive compounds in pollution.

MASSIVE ATTACK

Free radicals bang about in your cells, damaging DNA and other structures until they break down or are mopped up by the cell's protective machinery. The more free radicals you're exposed to, the more damage they'll do to your cells, and the quicker you'll age. According to one estimate, your body has to deal with around 10 trillion free radical "hits" per day! Smoking, taking drugs, and exposure to sunlight or pollution can boost this considerably. Eating healthy foods high in vitamins and minerals can provide you with antioxidants that help to mop up free radicals, reducing your biological age.

INTERPRETING THE SCORE

If your partner's lifestyle and history racked up more than 22 points on this checklist, he or she could have a biological age that is considerably older than his or her chronological age. This might have significant consequences for your relationship – are you likely to be happy with someone who is damaging their health and aging at an accelerated rate?

One way to answer this question is to go through the checklist for yourself. If you get a low score you're obviously someone who keeps an eye on health and lifestyle issues and who is therefore aging at a slower rate, in biological terms.

If this suggests a mismatch with your partner, don't panic! Many of the biological aging factors described above are ones you and your partner can do something about, drastically reducing biological aging. Most of the measures you can take are simple common sense – give up smoking, stay out of the sun, get lots of exercise, eat a healthy diet, and get to bed earlier most nights.

Are Your Sleeping Styles Compatible?

You will spend a third of your life asleep – the equivalent of 122 days every year. Since you're in a relationship, you either already spend most of that time lying next to your partner, or are planning to start doing so in the future. In other words, you and your partner will spend more time sleeping next to one another than doing any other shared activity, making the practicalities of sleep one of the most important issues in your relationship.

The Questionnaire

You will need to do this quiz together because you may not be properly aware of your own sleeping habits. Answer the questions and add up your score as you go along. Bear in mind that some questions should only be answered if you've given specific answers to previous questions.

1 Are you a heavy or light sleeper?
Heavy: 0 points; Light: 1 point

2 Is your partner a heavy or light sleeper?
Heavy: 0 points; Light: 1 point

3 Do you snore (sometimes/a bit/quietly)?
Yes: 1 point; No: 0 points

4 Does your partner snore (sometimes/a bit/quietly)?
Yes: 1 point; No: 0 points

5 Do you snore (loudly)?
Yes: 2 points; No: 0 points

6 Does your partner snore (loudly)?
Yes: 2 points; No: 0 points

7 Do you/your partner talk/walk in your sleep on a regular basis?
Yes: 2 points; No: 0 points

8 If "Yes" to any of Qs 3–7, answer this question: Are you/your partner sensitive to noise when sleeping?
Yes: 2 points; No: 0 points

9 Do you ever have a tug of war over sheets?

Yes: 1 point; No: 0 points

10 Do you like to lie against your partner when sleeping?

Does your partner like to lie against you while sleeping?

Answers agree: 0 points; Answers disagree: 2 points

11 Do you or your partner move around a lot during sleep?

Yes: 1 point; No: 0 points

12 Do you or your partner fidget and fuss a lot before you can get comfortable?

Yes: 1 point; No: 0 points

13 Does one of you like to go to sleep watching TV/listening to the radio, while the other doesn't?

Yes: 2 points; No: 0 points

14 Is one of you significantly heavier than the other?

Yes: 1 point; No: 0 points

15 Does one of you get up frequently during the night?

Yes: 1 point; No: 0 points

16 Does one of you keep to an odd sleep schedule (due to shift work, insomnia, being on call etc)?

Yes: 2 points; No: 0 points

17 Does one of you habitually come to bed later than the other?

Yes: 1 point; No: 0 points

INTERPRETING THE RESULTS

0–5 Your sleeping habits match up perfectly with your partner's, ensuring sweet sleep all night long.

6–14 A few disturbed nights may be yours, but the consequences are more likely to be mild irritation than despair. Pick the issue that bothers you most and work on that one first.

15–22 Stormy nights ahead! Bedroom battles can have dire consequences for your mental and physical functioning – fatigue causes impaired concentration and memory, learning difficulties, mental slowness, and impaired reactions, coordination, and movement. It also causes irritability, making fights more likely. You need to sort this out!

WHAT TO DO ABOUT A MISMATCH

Fortunately there are a number of concrete solutions to bedtime blues:

- **A bigger, better bed with a quality mattress** – this will make you both more comfortable and reduce bed vibration when one or other of you moves.
- **Individual mattresses so that each side is independent** – fussing and fidgeting from one side of the bed will stay there.
- **Soundproofing** – if outside noise is disturbing you, causing you to disturb your partner, sort it out.
- **Apnoea counseling** – snoring can be harmful to the snorer as well as the snoree. It can cause sleep apnoea, where oxygen supply to the brain is intermittently cut off. Counseling and, in drastic cases, surgery can help both of you.
- **Relaxation before bedtime** – if you have problems getting to sleep or are constantly getting up during the night, it could be because of stress and tension. Try relaxation exercises to reduce stress and improve sleep and you will both benefit.
- **Keep the bedroom for sleep and sex only** – TV, radio and the like can cause stress and prevent relaxation. Make your bedroom a haven.
- **Regular bedtimes for both of you** – get into regular sleeping habits and keep to them.

PART TWO

Are You Sexually Compatible?

When couples face issues about their sexual incompatibility it can feel very alarming. Should the problems not be resolved, for instance, if one of the partners complains of "poor sex," this a strong predictor of divorce. Sexual compatibility is a complex issue, involving much more than simply how often you make love or how many sexual positions you adopt. It's an issue that always needs to be explored.

Who says sex is so important?

YOU do! The evidence for the significance of sex is considerable. A range of surveys and studies shows that sexual satisfaction correlates strongly with marital satisfaction. Also, sexual satisfaction can be used to predict the likelihood of long-term relationship success. Interestingly, the same is not true of sexual frequency; having regular sex does not correlate strongly with marital satisfaction. Only when other issues, such as arguments, are factored in, can frequency of sex be used to predict marital satisfaction and relationship success. For example, if you have infrequent sex but few major fights the future still looks pretty bright, whereas frequent sex plus frequent serious rows indicates a less optimistic outcome. To couples at the start of a relationship this may seem counter-intuitive because one way in which they express their burgeoning physical and emotional intimacy is in frequent lovemaking – it feels as if the more they have sex, the more they are in love. Yet over the longer term, successful couples find that sexual satisfaction is very different – what really matters is to have quality sex, rather than try to get into the *Guinness Book of Records*.

The cement in your relationship

For individuals, sex is a basic drive, but for a couple it means much more than that. Sex is often described as the superglue that binds relationships – without it they fall apart. The key here is that sex also represents love-play-making. This complex activity between partners is an expression and reaffirmation of affection, intimacy, and attraction. It strengthens what biologists call the primary pair-bond. If such activity becomes unsatisfactory these powerful and important emotions are drained. When lovemaking remains good or improves, then whatever else a relationship is going through the partners can feel that they enjoy a secure foundation.

Successful sex

Couples who maintain successful long-term relationships are often those who maintain high levels of sexual compatibility. When talking about their sex lives such couples typically report that sex is much more relaxed, more fun, more satisfying, and more meaningful than for couples who are unhappy or who are having problems. Not all such couples maintain highly active sex lives, but even when they don't, the key fact is that they share the same sexual expectations. Even couples no longer having any sex can count themselves as "sexually compatible" if their celibacy is genuinely a mutually preferred option.

How can you measure sexual compatibility?

The best predictors of your sexual compatibility in the long term are your underlying attitudes, experience, and approach, plus how well these match with those of your partner. These factors relate to how comfortable you will feel with one another, how your sex life will affect your self-esteem, whether you both like / want the same things in bed, how you will deal with changes in your sex life over time, and how much such changes will matter to you both: all the elements of harmonious sex.

What's in this section

The six tests determining sexual compatibility examine your sexual experience, your sexual attitudes, your fidelity beliefs, your comfort with sexual discussion, your sex drive (or libido), and your sexual style.

Do Your Sexual Histories Match?

Research shows that, in general, people are more comfortable when their partners have had a similar sexual history to themselves. Men in particular, rate equivalent sexual experience as a major compatibility issue – according to research by a top internet dating agency, this is one of the top factors affecting male mate choice.

Many people find it difficult to talk to their partners about their own sexual histories. Maybe you're embarrassed about how many or how few lovers you've had. Maybe you imagine it reflects badly on you if you lost your virginity "too" early or late. Often partners don't want to disclose too much too early in a relationship. Then later, it can seem too late to come clean about facts you know your partner might not like. But your sexual past influences your sexual present, helping form your attitudes, anxieties, turn-ons, and hang-ups. Inevitably, the way your sexual history compares with your partner's makes a big impact on your sexual future. The questionnaire below lets you explore an honest and open comparison of sexual histories.

The Questionnaire

1 At what age did you lose your virginity?

a   *15 or younger.*

b   *16–20*

c   *21+*

2 How many sexual partners have you had in your life, before you met your current partner?

a   *None–2*

b   *3–10*

c   *11+*

3 How many of those were one-night-stands, as opposed to serious relationships?

a   *None.*

b   *1–5*

c   *5+*

4 Have you had any homosexual leanings, experiences, or encounters?

a   *No, never.*

b   *Only very minor / drunken experiences that didn't count.*

c   *Yes.*

5 Have you ever had any unpleasant, frightening, or abusive experiences?

a   *No, never.*

b   *Yes, but nothing too bad (a man exposed himself to me; a stranger touched my leg).*

c   *Yes.*

6 Have you ever had a sexually transmitted disease?

a   *No, never.*

b   *Not certain.*

c   *Yes.*

WHAT TO DO ABOUT A MISMATCH

Unequal sexual histories can become a major source of discontent in a relationship, and can end up used as weapons during arguments. Logically or not, the partner with the less "colorful" history may feel somehow inadequate or prudish, if only subconsciously. Conversely, the more adventurous partner may be afflicted with feelings of guilt or shame. In both cases, unpleasant feelings like this can in turn lead to feelings of resentment – "Why should I feel bad that I've slept with a few more people … just because he's inexperienced?"

Ultimately, the impact of mismatching sexual histories is a very personal thing. If you are a relaxed, self-confident person who feels secure and loved in your relationship, it's unlikely to matter much. But if your relationship has other problems then mismatching sexual histories can account for some of the difficulties.

Finally, your sexual histories also reveal a lot about your attitudes to sex and relationships in general, attitudes that affect your long-term compatibility.

The key to dealing with any potential sources of sexual strife is communication; you can overcome most problems by talking them through frankly and sensitively, following the Rules of Constructive Discussion (pages 154–5). Moreover, bear in mind the following:

- You are talking about today – you can't change yesterday.
- However, you can agree that there is more than one version of your shared history.
- People change; your partner's past is neither a comment on nor a criticism of you – it's just history.

INTERPRETING THE RESULTS

Close match You and your partner both got more than four As or more than four Cs.

Intermediate match More than four of your answers are within one place of each other (you said "A", your partner said "B"; or your partner said "C" and you said "B"). Where one of you has an "A" and the other one has a "C", your sexual histories start to look incompatible.

Mismatch More than four of your answers fall into opposing categories; you could have challenges ahead. Questions 4, 5, and 6, in particular, raise important issues. If your partner's answers surprised you, you may eventually need to address your attitudes.

How open-minded are you? How relaxed are you about sexual experimentation? How willing are you to push the boundaries of your emotional experience? These are issues that relate to your sexual "adventurousness."

This questionnaire looks at issues of open-mindedness and adventurousness, which relate to a dimension of sexual attitude labelled "permissiveness" by some researchers. For example, research has shown (not too surprisingly) that the higher you score on the permissiveness dimension the more partners you are likely to have had, and the greater the

variety of sexual practices you will have tried. In this way, then, open-mindedness is likely to have affected your sexual experience.

It also affects your sexual future. Long-term sexual satisfaction involves maintaining sexual interest and feeling that you are exploring your full sexual potential. This is only possible with someone who matches your attitudes to sex. Use this quiz to see if that person is your partner.

The Questionnaire

For questions 1–9, note your response to the suggested scenario by choosing one option from this scale:

1 Very interested/turned on
2 Quite interested/mildly aroused
3 Neutral/Don't mind one way or the other
4 Not interested
5 Shocked/disgusted

1 Your partner admits to being aroused by dressing up in your clothes/underwear.

| 1 | 2 | 3 | 4 | 5 |

2 You're visiting your partner at work and he/she leads you to a secluded room and suggests having sex.

| 1 | 2 | 3 | 4 | 5 |

3 Your partner suggests introducing a sex aid (a vibrator or dildo) into your lovemaking.

| 1 | 2 | 3 | 4 | 5 |

4 Your partner suggests that you swap traditional gender sex roles during lovemaking.

| 1 | 2 | 3 | 4 | 5 |

5 Your partner asks you to indulge in some light bondage (tying to bed with silk scarf, using a blindfold, wearing rubber clothes).

| 1 | 2 | 3 | 4 | 5 |

6 Your partner admits that he/she enjoys anal sex.

| 1 | 2 | 3 | 4 | 5 |

7 Your partner suggests that you watch each other masturbate as part of your foreplay.

| 1 | 2 | 3 | 4 | 5 |

8 Someone you find attractive says he/she would be interested in a threesome with you and your partner.

| 1 | 2 | 3 | 4 | 5 |

9 You and your partner are having sex behind a sand dune on a secluded beach when you realize that another couple have started doing the same thing within your line of vision.

| 1 | 2 | 3 | 4 | 5 |

For questions 10–15, follow the same principle using this scale:

1 Completely unfazed, totally comfortable/approve
2 It doesn't bother you that much but you wouldn't shout about it
3 Mildly embarrassed but what people do is their own business
4 Uncomfortable/mildly disapproving
5 Outraged/disgusted

10 Your partner admits that during his/her youth, a long time before you met, he/she took part in an "orgy."

| 1 | 2 | 3 | 4 | 5 |

11 You're staying with one set of parents and during the night you hear the unmistakable sounds of lovemaking coming from their bedroom.

| 1 | 2 | 3 | 4 | 5 |

12 A gay couple move in next door and you see them smooching in the garden.

| 1 | 2 | 3 | 4 | 5 |

13 One of your friends admits that she and her partner enjoy "swinging."

| 1 | 2 | 3 | 4 | 5 |

14 You're a houseguest staying in your 16-year-old niece's room when you discover a packet of condoms in her closet.

| 1 | 2 | 3 | 4 | 5 |

15 You're cleaning in your 18-year-old son's room when you come across a dildo.

| 1 | 2 | 3 | 4 | 5 |

INTERPRETING THE RESULTS

Total up the figures you gave in response to each question to get an individual rating, and get your partner to do the same. Now calculate the difference between the scores – this is your compatibility rating for sexual adventurousness.

0–20 Close match. You and your partner have similar attitudes towards sex and you are likely to have similar responses to sexual novelty or challenges. In the long run you are likely to feel comfortable with one another's sexuality and as a result more comfortable with your own.

21–40 Intermediate compatibility. In some areas one of you takes the lead and the other follows, while in other areas there is an uncomfortable difference between you. Some areas may be altogether taboo.

41–75 Low compatibility. One of you is much more open-minded and adventurous than the other. The more open-minded partner may feel frustrated, restricted, and even bored, while the less adventurous one could end up feeling hurt, resentful, and insecure.

WHAT TO DO ABOUT A MISMATCH

Overcoming deep-seated disagreements about sex and sexuality requires a very sensitive approach (see the Rules of Constructive Discussion pages 154–5).

Avoid confrontational remarks such as "You won't try anything" or "You're disgusting." Start off by discussing why you feel certain things are OK or improper. One of the main dangers in cases of mismatching adventurousness is that the less adventurous partner feels threatened by the suggestions/desires of the other partner – that they indicate a lack of respect, a desire for someone else, or an implied criticism. These fears must be tackled before you can start to talk about trying new things. If you do reach a point where you can suggest something new, proceed very carefully. The less confident partner must feel in control. It can be useful to agree an "exit word" beforehand – a word that either partner can use to stop things if he/she feels uncomfortable.

Most people are fairly clear about their attitude to infidelity in a partner – it's generally unacceptable. So it may seem that this test is somewhat redundant.

However, social attitudes to fidelity tend to change with age in two directions. First, some young liberal types tend to be "polyamorous" – believing it is possible, for example, to love two people at the same time. Second, those in relationships that have lasted for many years may feel more tolerant of the odd "lapse of judgment." In all cases, however, what you and your partner must define is the nature of infidelity for *you*, because there's more to this issue than simply having sex with another person. This test looks at perceptions of behavior and examines the subtler shades of gray that can cause misunderstandings between partners with mismatching attitudes about what constitutes infidelity.

Your conception of fidelity affects both your behavior and your perception of your partner's. Rigid conceptions of fidelity place more demands on a relationship because these set higher standards. But high standards, by their nature, are more likely not to be met. If your attitudes to fidelity match, however, you will probably understand what your other half expects and how he/she perceives your behavior. Then, both of you will agree with those standards and behave accordingly.

The Test

This is a quiz for both partners. For questions 1–5, give your reaction, on a scale of 0 to 10, to the following scenarios:

0	1	2	3	4	5	6	7	8	9	10

not remotely bothered   want to show him/her the door

1 You are having a heated discussion with an attractive person of the same gender as yourself – your partner supports the views of that person.

0	1	2	3	4	5	6	7	8	9	10

2 You catch your partner looking at pornography.

0	1	2	3	4	5	6	7	8	9	10

3 Your partner has a friend with whom the pair of you frequently socialize. Not until you've been together for some time, however, do you discover that they slept together before you came on the scene.

0	1	2	3	4	5	6	7	8	9	10

4 Your partner makes admiring comments about an attractive television celebrity.

0	1	2	3	4	5	6	7	8	9	10

5 You discover that last week your partner was taken along to a strip club and ended up putting some money in the stripper's thong.

0	1	2	3	4	5	6	7	8	9	10

For questions 6–10, use the same scale to rate how much jealousy you think it would be reasonable for your partner to show in the given scenario:

6 While out on the town without your partner you bump into an ex (one who has a new partner of his/her own) and end up going for dinner together.

0 1 2 3 4 5 6 7 8 9 10

7 You admit to having briefly kissed someone you don't find remotely attractive at a very drunken Christmas party – your partner knows how drunk you were and you've apologized until you're blue in the face.

0 1 2 3 4 5 6 7 8 9 10

8 You're going on a girls/boys-only night out and tell your partner you'll be back by 11:30, but don't crawl in until 4 in the morning.

0 1 2 3 4 5 6 7 8 9 10

9 Your partner catches you ogling an attractive person walking by when you are on the beach together.

0 1 2 3 4 5 6 7 8 9 10

10 You and your partner are out at a party and you spend a large chunk of the night talking to a friendly person of the opposite sex.

0 1 2 3 4 5 6 7 8 9 10

INTERPRETING THE RESULTS

Total up your ratings and compare your score to your partner's – the difference is your fidelity compatibility rating.

0–30 Compatible. You and your partner shouldn't have too much trouble with jealousy, either because you are not very jealous people or because you both avoid situations that might give rise to suspicion.

31–60 Some incompatibility. You may not always agree on what constitutes an acceptable response to ambiguous behavior, but you do share similar ideas about how to behave.

61–100 Incompatible. You have very different ideas about what constitutes acceptable behavior. Fights seem inevitable, with one partner making accusations of betrayal and infidelity and the other of unreasonable behavior and over-reaction.

WHAT TO DO ABOUT A MISMATCH

Constant problems with jealousy and fears of infidelity are often signs that one partner is suffering from low self-esteem and feels insecure. Overcoming these problems requires sensitivity and the correct level of reassurance. Jealousy is a normal emotion if there is evidence of betrayal. However, jealousy can become pathological when used to mask anxiety or a troubling personal history of relationship disaster and rejection. Constant reassurance is counter-productive in the latter case. It is better to try to link the feelings of insecurity to the actual events before you came on the scene and get your partner to open up. The jealous partner needs to articulate his/her feelings in a non-accusatory way, while the other partner must ensure that his/her love is made explicit.

• Use "I feel…" to preface statements so that they are less aggressive/accusatory.

• Don't assume that your positive regard for each other can be left unspoken – make sure you say it out loud!

• Some clinical psychologists suggest recasting jealousy as a challenge to strengthen your relationship instead of something that undermines it.

Good communication is the key to overcoming sexual problems and improving compatibility. To cope with sexual issues (from mismatching libido to clashing sexual styles) you have to be able to talk about them. But how good are you at discussing sexual matters with your partner? Do you spell out rude words in stage whispers or chat happily about the most personal bodily functions?

The Questionnaire

The aim here is to discover which style of bedroom communication you use. Try wherever possible to relate the scenarios described to real events that have happened to you and your partner, so that your answer shows not just what you would do but what you actually did.

1 **During sex your partner reaches orgasm first and then stops and wants to snuggle. You feel a bit frustrated but your partner doesn't seem to be picking up on it. What do you do?**

a   *It would be too awkward to come out and say, "I want an orgasm too," so you carry on trying to let your body do the talking.*

b   *Use some encouraging phrases like "Don't stop — I'm so turned on" or "That was so good, I want more."*

c   *Your partner wouldn't react well to demands so you try to forget about an orgasm and throw yourself into the cuddling.*

d   *Tell your partner straight that you're not yet satisfied.*

2 **Your partner is tired after a long day at work and needs to relax, but you are in a frisky mood so you keep on trying to arouse him/her. How would your partner react?**

a   *Gently explain the situation and offer lots of reassurances that it's not because he/she doesn't find you attractive.*

b   *Snap at you.*

c   *Try and deflect your attentions by changing the subject.*

d   *Do his/her best to get into the mood too.*

3 **Although you're both aroused and want to have sex, your partner experiences some sort of problem (such as losing erection, or not becoming lubricated enough) and you have to stop. What's your reaction?**

a   *You shouldn't dwell on these things because then they get blown out of proportion.*

b   *Be supportive and understanding but not go on about it.*

c   *There's obviously a problem of some sort and it needs to be addressed or it might recur.*

d   *Don't say anything directly, but hug and cuddle your partner to show it doesn't matter.*

4 **You feel unwell, but know that your partner is expecting a night of passion. How would the situation most likely be handled?**

a   *Excuses along the lines of "I don't feel like it" would be made, but no details would be given.*

b   *Say nothing and hope you can last out.*

c   *The problem would be described and discussed.*

d   *Appropriate arrangements (such as a bucket by the side of the bed) would be made without further comment.*

5 **If you and your partner used condoms as a contraceptive, but you discovered that one had split during sex, how would you both deal with it?**

a *Avoid the subject and leave the outcome to fate.*

b *There'd be much agonizing and discussion before a joint arrangement is made.*

c *One of you would try to talk about it but the other would just rather deal with it without a fuss.*

c *Options would be discussed but ultimately it would be up to the woman to seek medical help.*

6 **Which of the following characteristics does your partner demonstrate when the two of you are talking about sex or intimate matters?**

a *Over-analysis, tendency to interrupt, tendency to go into graphic detail, patronizing manner.*

b *Embarrassment, disapproval, reticence, impatience.*

c *Slight discomfort, easily distracted.*

c *Maturity, willingness, a sense of humor.*

Work out your scores by using the table to see which letter your answer corresponds to – W, X, Y, or Z – and total up the number of times you get each letter. Then do the same for your partner.

Question/Answer	a	b	c	d
1	Y	Z	X	W
2	Z	W	Y	X
3	X	Z	W	Y
4	X	Y	W	Z
5	Y	W	X	Z
6	W	X	Y	Z

INTERPRETING THE RESULTS

Each of the four letters – W, X, Y, or Z – corresponds to a style of communication used in relationships. Which did you get most?

W You like to be totally frank and truthful with one another – but you risk being insensitive, boorish, aggressive, and patronizing.

X You feel uncomfortable unless sexual matters are kept under wraps, but a buttoned-up style means that you could be repressing feelings and suppressing important discussions.

Y You tend to think that what's left unsaid won't cause problems, but this head-in-the-sand approach means that serious issues won't get dealt with, simply pushed away and left to grow worse.

Z You and your partner are open with each other but also sensitive and tactful. This is the style that makes for the greatest sexual compatibility over the course of a long relationship.

WHAT TO DO ABOUT A MISMATCH

If your partnership falls into the W, X, or Y categories, you both need to work on your communication techniques. Here are some simple rules:

• If you find it hard to talk about sexual issues because of embarrassment or discomfort, try to discover why and discuss it (e.g. it was a taboo subject when you were growing up).

• Set aside special times and even places for "difficult" discussions. A special setting can give you "permission" to talk about things you wouldn't normally. It may help to sit in the dark, for example.

• Become better listeners by making sure you allow each other to speak uninterrupted and that your answers to your partner's statements acknowledge and respond to what he/she has just said directly and explicitly.

• Be positive, supportive, and encouraging in all your statements and responses.

Do Your Libidos Match?

Lovemaking is powered by the drive for love, sex, and life – literally by your libido. To make an analogy with an airplane, what makes your craft soar into the sky is the power in its engines – how much "oomph" it possesses. Stretching the analogy a little, we can apply the same logic to lovers. To a large extent, what determines whether two people are sexually compatible is the strength of their respective libidos. Your libido is what determines how frisky you feel in the morning, how many times you like to do it in a night, and whether you'd rather settle down with a good book and a cup of cocoa instead. Obviously, matching libidos are important to sexual compatibility.

The concept of libido or sex drive was formulated by the Viennese analyst Sigmund Freud as part of his theory about the unconscious forces underlying human motivation. He argued that the libido, which he eventually expanded to mean "life force" in general, was the seat of all human creativity. Nowadays, we're not quite as hung up on sex as Freud, but the libido remains a recognized concept in sexual psychology. In some ways it's more important than ever, because the most common sexual dysfunction treated by therapists today is lack of sexual desire, otherwise known as "diminished libido." We also know a lot more about the influence of hormones on libido – specifically testosterone. Although this is best known as a male sex hormone it is present in both genders and plays a role in controlling libido. Obviously, carrying out blood tests for hormone levels are beyond the scope of a book, so the following quiz seeks to assess your libido in other ways.

The Questionnaire

Both you and your partner should answer the questions and work out libido scores.

1 Your partner's been away on a two-week trip. When he/she gets home do you:

a *Peck your partner on the cheek and tell him/her about your day.*

b *Tear off your partner's clothes as soon as he/she walks in the door and drag him/her to bed?*

c *Look forward to showing your partner just how much you missed him/her later on that evening?*

2 It's Sunday morning, there's no one at home except you and your partner, and you've got nothing to do and no one to see all day. Ideally, what would you like to get up to?

a *Spend most of the day in bed being physically intimate.*

b *Spend most of the day in bed sleeping or reading the papers.*

c *Get up bright and early to do some work or errands.*

3 Your partner's treated you to an indulgent weekend away. One evening, after covering you with baby oil he/she gives you a sensual massage. What do you do afterward?

a *Have a shower and join your partner for a romantic dinner.*

b *Have a doze.*

c *Have friction-free, slippery sex.*

4 You're running late for work and you know colleagues will be waiting for you, but your partner's woken up with a glint in his/her eye and a come-hither voice. What do you do?

a   *Call in sick for the morning and get back into bed.*
b   *Shed your clothes for a quickie.*
c   *Get cross and get going.*

5 What scenario best describes your idea of a perfect romantic weekend away together?

a   *Antique shops, candlelit dinners, moonlit strolls, and slow, gentle lovemaking.*
b   *Invigorating walks through beautiful countryside and exciting activities (e.g. hang-gliding, water-skiing, snowboarding) that leave you delightfully exhausted at the end of the day.*
c   *A night of passion followed by a morning of bedroom playfulness, with a lunchtime excursion for sustenance followed by some afternoon romping.*

INTERPRETING THE RESULTS

Work out your libido score using the table below. Now compare your score to your partner's and calculate the difference – this is your libido compatibility rating.

Question/Answer	a	b	c
1	0	4	2
2	4	0	0
3	2	0	4
4	4	2	0
5	2	0	4

Difference 0–9 You and your partner have similar needs and levels of desire. When it comes to sex you generally want the same thing at the same time and are able to respond to each other's advances or lack of them.

Difference 10–20 Your sexual motor seems to be running at a different speed to your partner's. One of you wants a lot more sex than the other and the consequent disparity could put a strain on your relationship.

WHAT TO DO ABOUT A MISMATCH

First of all, don't panic if your relationship fails this test, because while it carries weight in the present, it's predictive ability over the long-term isn't foolproof. This is because libido changes with age and within a relationship. In the short-term, however, a mismatch needs to be dealt with. One possible solution is a "sex contract:"

• Each partner has three nights of the week when he/she can decide whether or not to have sex, and the other partner must abide by that.

• On the seventh night both partners decide whether or not they want to have sex.

• Whoever decides not to have sex must make sure his/her decision is not seen as a rejection.

• Explore non-sexual alternatives such as caressing.

The key element of a great sex life and the ultimate arbiter of sexual compatibility is whether or not you and your partner have congenial sexual styles. All the factors examined in this section feed into sexual style, so in a way, this test is a summary of all the issues underlying sexual compatibility.

Your sexual style is a way of describing not just your behavior in the bedroom but also your approach to sex – the type of sexual practices you enjoy, how adventurous you are,

your sexual response, and your libido. Finding a sexually compatible partner doesn't necessarily mean finding someone with exactly the same style, although generally that does lead to great sex. Different styles can match or complement one another, with the same result. When styles are identical, naturally they match. But if one is more dominant while the other is more submissive, you also may have the makings of a perfect situation.

The Test

Dividing sexual styles into categories is arbitrary, but for the purposes of this exercise I've drawn up a list of characteristic styles. Go through the list and choose just one category that comes closest to a description of your style. Then get your partner to do the same. Use the table opposite to see how well your styles match up.

Category D
You often initiate sex and are quite **dominant**/aggressive in bed (you like to decide which positions you adopt, when to change position, etc. Often you like to be on top and in control).

Category E
You are a smooth, **experienced** lover who is technically adept. You are adaptable in the bedroom, have few hang-ups, and enjoy a range of practices and styles – you expect the same from your partner.

Category F
You laugh a lot in the bedroom and enjoy **fooling around** and cracking jokes. Sex should be fun – you find it hard to take it seriously.

Category H
You are an athletic, sporty, **high-energy** lover who takes sex quite seriously and thinks that if you're not working up a sweat you're obviously not doing it properly.

Category K
You can be quite **kinky** and enjoy experimenting and pushing the boundaries of your sexuality.

Category I
You are a slightly timid lover who is sometimes afraid of getting it wrong. Your **inexperience** makes you reluctant to let yourself go in case you embarrass yourself or are caught out.

Category L
You can get pretty wild in the bedroom and can be **loud** in your lovemaking. You are undoubtedly passionate, but at times also a little theatrical.

Category R
You like to be comfortable in the bedroom, to **relax** and enjoy taking things slowly. You prefer sex to be a sensual, languorous experience.

Category S
You are quite passive in bed and naturally fall into a more **submissive** role, letting your partner take the lead and dictate how your lovemaking unfolds.

Category T
You are a bit of a **traditionalist** in the bedroom and like each partner to follow typical gender roles. You aren't comfortable with new-fangled ideas about who should be doing what.

COMPATIBILITY MATRIX

Female / Male	D	E	F	H	K	I	L	R	S	T
D	○▼	○	▼	○	○❖	▼	○	▼	❖	❖
E	○▼	❖	○▼	○	○▼	○	○	○	▼	○
F	○▼	○▼	❖	○▼	○	○▼	❖	○▼	▼	▼
H	❖	○	○▼	❖	▼	▼	❖	▼	▼	○▼
K	○❖	○▼	○	▼	❖	▼	○▼	▼	○❖	▼
I	▼	○	○▼	▼	▼	▼	▼	○	▼	○
L	○	○	❖	○	○▼	▼	❖	▼	○	▼
R	▼	○	○▼	▼	▼	○	▼	❖	○▼	○
S	❖	○	▼	▼	○❖	▼	○▼	○▼	▼	▼
T	▼	▼	▼	▼	▼	○	▼	○▼	❖	❖

KEY

▼ **Mismatch**

○ **Well-matched**

❖ **Very well-matched**

○❖ **Well-matched and potentially very well-matched ***

○▼ **Depends/could go either way ****

Depending on personal variables – a kinky lover and a submissive lover (K/S) might get along famously if the latter is sufficiently submissive and the former into S&M.

**Again, personal variables are all-important, making it hard to generalize. For example, D/D – some dominant/aggressive-style lovers enjoy a partner who also takes the initiative, but others will feel that they're in a power struggle; K/F – some experimental lovers appreciate a partner who can laugh about their kinkier ideas, but others might take themselves more seriously.*

INTERPRETING THE RESULTS

Use the chart to find you and your partner's styles, then follow the two lines until you come to the box common to you both. Within is the symbol that shows whether you match or not.

WHAT TO DO ABOUT A MISMATCH

This is not an exact science, especially since sexual styles can and do change with time. People often end up gravitating towards styles such as R and away from styles such as H.

Partners with mismatching styles often end up having a sort of lowest-common-denominator-sex-life-by-tacit-agreement. If this applies to you, you need to talk openly with your partner about your respective needs and styles (see the Rules of Constructive Discussion, pages 154–5). If you handle each other properly, you can learn to loosen up your sexual preferences and adapt to one another's styles. Try to focus less on your differences and more on the positive aspects of your shared eroticism.

PART THREE

Are You Psychologically Compatible?

What do you and your partner spend most of your time doing? Chances are it's not making love, no matter how lusty you are. The duration of sex in most relationships takes from five to 20 minutes – an average of up to one hour a week. The major part of your time together is spent in similar ways to the time you spend with friends: talking, hanging out, just being together. To sustain this in the long-term it's vital that you and your partner gel; that you like each other and enjoy each other's company; that you think and feel in similar ways. In other words, that you are psychologically compatible – not just on your first date or for the first month, but over years and decades.

The term we use to refer to the long-term psychological characteristics of an individual is personality – the sum of the person's relatively stable and long-lasting characteristics (also known as traits). Psychological compatibility is determined by how well your personality matches your partner's. In order to assess it in depth, you need to look at the various elements.

Traits and tests

The psychology of personality is a contentious field because there is limited agreement over the definition of the various traits and drawing up a list of the characteristics that make up your personality is difficult. Some characteristics of behavior are common to practically all humans but are not very informative. For example, the ability to use language is a defining feature of human psychology, but not necessarily of your personality. Other characteristics depend more on the situation you find yourself in. You may feel frightened watching a horror movie, but being frightened isn't necessarily part of your personality.

Even characteristics that are generally agreed on can run into trouble, because it's hard to say which traits are separate from others, or simply make up facets of a more general trait. For instance, shyness, dislike of crowds, enjoyment of solitude, thoughtfulness, hesitancy when speaking, modesty, deference, and timidity are all different but interconnected traits. In the case of this particular list, psychologists say that these are all aspects of the over-arching personality trait introversion.

Introversion itself is the opposite of extraversion, which involves being gregarious, outgoing, confident, sociable, boastful, brash, etc. Most people fall somewhere between these two extremes. Therefore, we can say that extraversion/introversion forms one personality dimension.

How many other dimensions are there? Different theories say there are anywhere between one and dozens, but the general consensus is that there are five main personality dimensions:

- Extraversion vs introversion
- Conscientiousness/responsibility vs irresponsibility
- Openness/imagination vs lack of imagination
- Agreeableness vs irritability
- Neuroticism/emotional stability vs instability

This section includes tests to see whether you and your partner are compatible on all five of these dimensions, together with some other elements of personality that are generally agreed upon. I've also included some less well recognized ones – emotional intelligence, creativity, sense of humor, and boredom threshold – because I know from my counseling experience that they are important to people. There also are tests that look at some of the aspects of your life that are most influenced by your personality, such as your likes and dislikes. Finally, I've included two tests that look directly at the effect that your personality has on the way you relate to your partner in arguments and in your everyday interactions.

Nature vs nurture

Where do the personality traits discussed above come from? Are they part of your genetic heritage – innate characteristics of your brain and therefore your psychology? Or are they the result of your upbringing and life experiences – learned or acquired characteristics? The answer is probably that personality comes from a combination of the two forces. However, since assessing the genetic input to your personality characteristics is beyond the scope of this book, the remaining tests in this section look at the "nurture" side of the equation, investigating your personal and family histories, and asking whether these match up with your partner's.

Are You an Extrovert or an Introvert?

Extroversion and its opposite introversion are thought to be one of the strongest dimensions of one's personality. The diagram (right) shows some of the characteristics, positive and negative, typically associated with it.

Some psychologists argue that extroversion–introversion is the most fundamental personality dimension, and that most or all of the other characteristics are aspects of it. Some argue that it must be biological – in other words, that shy people may have different brain structures than gregarious ones.

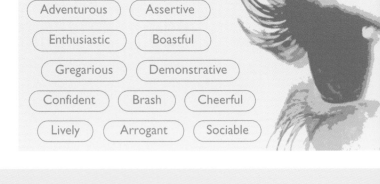

EXTROVERSION

Talkative

Adventurous · Assertive

Enthusiastic · Boastful

Gregarious · Demonstrative

Confident · Brash · Cheerful

Lively · Arrogant · Sociable

The Questionnaire

You and your partner should both complete this quiz and then compare results.

1 If you were at a party and someone wanted to take your picture how would you react?

a   *Hide your face to discourage them.*
b   *Smile and pose.*

2 You've gone to see a talk by your favorite author and there's a question you've always wanted to ask her. After her spiel she takes questions. Would you stand up and ask your question, or wait until afterward and try to approach her one-to-one?

a   *Wait until after the talk.*
b   *Stand up in front of everyone.*

3 Your boss gives you a choice of two projects to work on. One involves working on your own, the other means joining a team. Which do you choose?

a   *The one where you work as a team.*
b   *The one where you work on your own.*

4 Scanning the seating arrangements at a wedding reception you see that you've been placed between two strangers. What do you do?

a   *Sit down and introduce yourself to your neighbors — after all, a stranger's just a friend you haven't met.*
b   *Rearrange the name cards so you're seated with friends.*

5 You're at a stand-up comedy show but when the comic comes on you realize that you're in plain view and you *really* need a comfort break! What do you do?

a   *Cross your legs and wait for the intermission, even though you won't be able to laugh without endangering your pants.*
b   *Get up and go to the bathroom — let the comic do his worst!*

6 You're taking an evening class and the lecturer asks the class a question but no one seems to know the answer except you. Would you put your hand up?

a   *Yes.*
b   *No.*

7 Do you have lots of friends or a few very close ones?

a   *Lots.*
b   *A few close ones.*

INTROVERSION

Reserved

Introspective · Cautious

Modest · Unpretentious

Thoughtful · Stand-offish

Loner · Meek · Gloomy

Quiet · Timid · Shy

8 **At your annual review your boss tells you that you've been selected top employee for the whole company. How would you feel about telling your friends about it?**

a   *You wouldn't hide it, but you wouldn't specifically mention it.*

b   *You feel as though they should know.*

INTERPRETING THE RESULTS

Use this key to calculate your scores and then find the difference between the two. This is your compatibility rating for extroversion–introversion.

Question/Answer	a	b
1	0	1
2	0	1
3	1	0
4	1	0
5	0	1
6	1	0
7	0	1
8	1	0

0–2 You have a highly compatible extroversion–introversion dimension. Your temperaments match up perfectly in terms of gregariousness, sociability, volubility, etc.

3–5 You have intermediate compatibility. One of you may be louder, more outgoing, and demonstrative than the other. There will be times when the more introverted partner is embarrassed or irritated by the more extrovert, and times when the more extrovert will be exasperated or disappointed by the introvert.

6–8 You have low compatibility in this area. One of you likes meeting people and going to parties while the other likes to stay in and is shy of new people. One of you will heckle at a comedy show while the other will crawl under the seat. There is plenty of opportunity for conflict.

WHAT TO DO ABOUT A MISMATCH

It's a mystery how two people who are so different hooked up in the first place, but now that you've found each other do not despair! First of all, you'll have to overcome your gut reaction to the features in your partner that exasperate and irritate, whether you feel that your partner is too timid, gloomy, and sullen or too loud, arrogant, and showy. Remember, just because you don't agree with the way your partner handles certain things, it doesn't mean that way is wrong – just different.

Secondly, use your differences to your advantage by becoming complementary to one another. If your partner is extrovert he or she can help you to be more assertive, to meet people and come out of your shell, to take more enjoyment out of life. If your partner is an introvert, he or she can help you become more modest, appreciate the quiet pleasures of life, and keep your head down when necessary.

Conscientiousness is a later addition to the pantheon of what are known as cardinal personality traits, but it describes well a characteristic that most people can relate to, and one that is important to relationships. Conscientiousness or responsibility is at one end of a continuum, and the other end is irresponsibility. The diagram below shows some of the characteristics, positive and negative, typically associated with both.

Conscientiousness often correlates to birth order (see page 80) – first-born children traditionally score higher and last-borns lower. Does this match with your own family pattern?

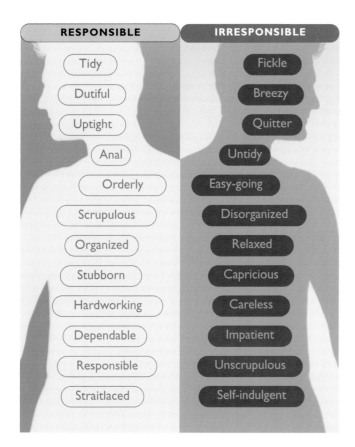

RESPONSIBLE	IRRESPONSIBLE
Tidy	Fickle
Dutiful	Breezy
Uptight	Quitter
Anal	Untidy
Orderly	Easy-going
Scrupulous	Disorganized
Organized	Relaxed
Stubborn	Capricious
Hardworking	Careless
Dependable	Impatient
Responsible	Unscrupulous
Straitlaced	Self-indulgent

The Questionnaire

You and your partner should both complete this quiz and then compare results.

1 Your birthday is coming up and one of your gifts arrives a week early, with "Do not open until your birthday!" written on the front of the card. Would you wait until your birthday or open it right away?
a   *Wait.*
b   *Open it right now.*

2 You've gone to see a "worthy" movie that all the critics have raved about. Halfway through you realize that you're bored. Would you walk out in the middle or stay until the end?
a   *Walk out in the middle.*
b   *Wait until the end.*

3 You're buying something at your neighborhood store and the cashier gives you your change. When you get outside you realize that he's given you a ten dollar bill instead of five dollars. Would you go back and return the extra money?
a   *Yes.*
b   *No.*

4 When you are given an assignment to complete at work or school, which of the following best describes your approach?
a   *Leave it until the last minute.*
b   *Get to work right away and keep working until it's finished.*

5 Which of the following statements do you agree with most?
a   *Rules are made to be broken.*
b   *You should never break the law.*

6 You've been told you have to do the monthly filing at work. It's tedious work. What sort of a job would you be most likely to do?

a *A thorough one, even if it takes a long time and means double-checking — any kind of job is worth doing well.*

b *A quick one — this is hardly important stuff, and a few mistakes won't hurt anyone.*

7 You are in a colleague's office and notice that her desk is neat and orderly, with no stray papers or pens lying about. What conclusion would you be most likely to draw?

a *She's anally retentive and needs to loosen up.*

b *She's neat and tidy — and that's commendable.*

8 You're baby-sitting for a friend who has given you strict instructions not to give the kids more than two cookies each and not to let them stay up past nine-thirty. The kids have other ideas and start begging for more. What would your reaction be?

a *A couple of cookies and an extra half-hour of fun aren't going to kill them.*

b *Their mother knows best and they should do as they're told.*

INTERPRETING THE RESULTS

Use this key to calculate your scores and then find the difference between the two. This is your compatibility rating for conscientiousness.

Question/Answer	a	b
1	1	0
2	0	1
3	1	0
4	0	1
5	0	1
6	1	0
7	0	1
8	0	1

0–2 If you both scored high you share similar approaches to following the rules, working hard, etc. If you both scored low you're unlikely to be disappointed in one another if you behave less than impeccably. However, you may both have suspect attitudes about issues such as fidelity, loyalty, etc.

3–5 You have intermediate compatibility. You may be set for the occasional argument over ethical issues and gratification delay.

6–8 You have low compatibility. One of you has much higher standards than the other, while one of you may think the other is a real goody-goody. This dimension affects your thinking about ethics, morals, and values, so you could find yourself at odds over many core values.

WHAT TO DO ABOUT A MISMATCH

It's important to remember that the difference between high and low conscientiousness is not necessarily the same as the difference between good and bad. People who differ on this dimension can compensate for each other's weaknesses, with the high-scorer helping the other to develop a bit of "stickability," and the low-scorer helping the other to loosen up a bit.

Are You Open to New Experiences?

Openness to experience, also known as imagination, deals with how adaptable a person's thinking is, how original and creative that person is, and the degree to which he/she is prepared to question or conform. The other end of this dimension is close-mindedness or lack of imagination. High scores for openness are generally associated with artistic and creative impulses (see page 70), liberal attitudes, and a desire to seek out the unfamiliar and look for complexity. Low scores are associated with conservative people who prefer to follow routines and stick to what they are comfortable with.

The diagram on the right shows some of the positive and negative characteristics typically associated with both ends of this dimension.

OPEN-MINDED

Independent · Imaginative · Creative · Unpredictable · Deep and complex thinker · Rebellious · Artistic · Tolerant of ambiguity · Nonconforming · Original · Liberal · Questioning

The Questionnaire

You and your partner should both complete this quiz and then compare results.

1 If the resort you went to last year was the best vacation of your life, would you go back to the same place this year or try somewhere different?
a   *Go back to the same place.*
b   *Try a different sort of vacation.*

2 Which of the following is closest to your ideal night out?
a   *A night spent with your friends at your favorite bar or restaurant.*
b   *Visiting a new night spot and meeting an interesting new crowd of people.*

3 Imagine that your child wanted to try a strange food combination, such as peanut butter on his spaghetti. What would you say?
a   *"Sounds horrible but go ahead and try it if you want!"*
b   *"No way!"*

4 You've been invited to your cousin's wedding, but she's decided to get married underwater in a swimming pool and all the guests have to wear swimming costumes and snorkels. Would you go?
a   *Sure — it sounds like fun.*
b   *Probably not — what's wrong with a traditional service?*

5 When you're watching the news, what sort of reporting do you prefer?
a   *Someone who analyzes the issues in depth and explores more than one angle.*
b   *Someone plain-speaking who lays out all the issues clearly and simply.*

6 You go to the movies to see a film that a friend has recommended, but in the lobby discover that it's a black-and-white foreign language documentary with subtitles. Would you go watch it?
a   *Yes.*
b   *Probably not.*

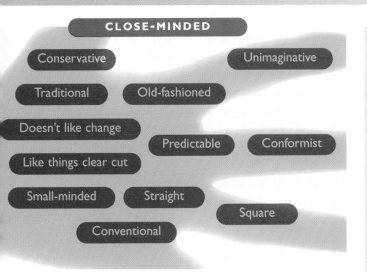

CLOSE-MINDED

Conservative
Unimaginative
Traditional
Old-fashioned
Doesn't like change
Predictable
Conformist
Like things clear cut
Small-minded
Straight
Square
Conventional

INTERPRETING THE RESULTS

Use this key to calculate your scores and then find the difference between the two. This is your compatibility rating for openness.

Question/Answer	a	b
1	0	1
2	0	1
3	1	0
4	1	0
5	1	0
6	1	0
7	1	0
8	0	1

0–2 High compatibility. Means that you're more likely to share interests, friends, political stance, etc.

3–5 Intermediate compatibility. There are bound to be some conflicts but these are made up for by the way that each of your strengths complements the other's weaknesses.

6–8 Low compatibility. There could be a real problem. One of you is traditional, the other is progressive. One of you is adventurous, the other is cautious. This limits your options for shared activities and interests.

WHAT TO DO ABOUT A MISMATCH

Scoring high on the openness dimension means that you're more likely to be able to understand where your less imaginative partner is coming from. If you can couple this with respect for his/her point of view you can overcome the distance between you. If, on the other hand, you are the more conservative partner, you may have to work harder to overcome your natural suspicion of your partner's freethinking, experimental attitudes. Focus on the positive aspects of being more open-minded – e.g., open-minded people are more open to opportunity. If all else fails, console yourself with the knowledge that open-mindedness generally decreases with age.

7 You're walking along the beach looking for a place to spread out your towel and catch a few rays. You see a vacant spot but then notice that right next to it are two people engaged in a heavy petting session. What do you do?

a *Unfold your towel and sit down.*

b *Look for another spot.*

8 It's lunchtime and you've joined dozens of other workers in eating your lunch in the local park. A couple of kids are doing skateboard tricks on and over the benches. What's your reaction?

a *Anger that their antisocial antics are inconveniencing others and might even hurt someone.*

b *Admiration of their skill.*

Perhaps the most intuitively obvious of the big five personality characteristics, agreeableness, has direct implications for relationships. It involves attitudes toward other people – trust, cooperation, and altruism. In layman's terms, someone who scores highly on this dimension might be described as "good-natured" or "nice." The opposite is antagonism, irritability, and selfishness.

This dimension strongly affects the type and tone of your relationships – whether they are friendly or hostile, easy-going or acrimonious. Obviously, people who score low on agreeableness are at greater risk of having arguments and breakups with partners. On the other hand, it could be argued that people who score highly are more at risk of being taken advantage of (although your view on this might depend on your score in this test).

The diagram below shows some of the characteristics, positive and negative, typically associated with these opposing traits.

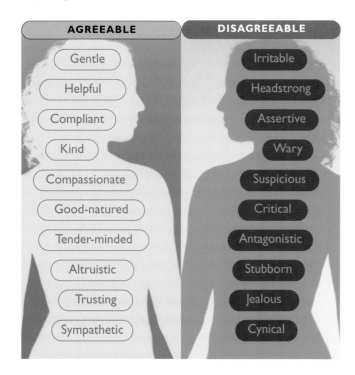

AGREEABLE	DISAGREEABLE
Gentle	Irritable
Helpful	Headstrong
Compliant	Assertive
Kind	Wary
Compassionate	Suspicious
Good-natured	Critical
Tender-minded	Antagonistic
Altruistic	Stubborn
Trusting	Jealous
Sympathetic	Cynical

The Questionnaire

You and your partner should both complete this quiz and then compare results.

1 **If you had an argument with a friend and then received a call from him/her what would your first thought be?**

a   *My friend wants to make up.*
b   *My friend wants to start another fight.*

2 **Imagine that a younger brother, cousin, or nephew is telling you a story and he mispronounces a word. What would you be most likely to do?**

a   *Correct him.*
b   *Ignore the mistake.*

3 **If someone cuts you off while you're driving what would you be most likely to do?**

a   *Show your irritation by honking your horn or tailgating.*
b   *Let it go.*

4 **You're at a party talking to a group of friends when a new person is introduced to your group. The newcomer starts to talk, rather loudly, about a recent trip to Africa. What's your first thought?**

a   *This person is pushy.*
b   *He/she must be nervous what with suddenly having to talk to a bunch of people who already know each other.*

5 **One of your colleagues keeps taking time off because of problems at home, but you have to pick up the slack at work. How do you feel?**

a   *Concerned about your colleague.*
b   *Irritated you have to suffer because of another person's problems.*

INTERPRETING THE RESULTS

Use this key to calculate your scores and then find the difference between the two. This is your rating on the agreeableness dimension.

Question/Answer	a	b
1	1	0
2	0	1
3	0	1
4	0	1
5	1	0
6	1	0
7	1	0
8	0	1

0–4 If you both scored high for agreeableness it bodes well for the future of the relationship – you both get along well with everyone. If you both scored low, however, your relationship might be more prickly and argumentative. But at least irritable, suspicious, cynical people understand each other.
5–8 Low compatibility on this dimension. One of you seems to be "nicer" than the other. Not every couple minds this, especially as part of being agreeable is making allowances for disagreeable people. Also, the more suspicious partner possibly prevents the other partner from being taken advantage of too often.

WHAT TO DO ABOUT A MISMATCH

Most of us would like to become "nicer" people, and your relationship offers one partner a model for achieving this. If you are the "disagreeable" partner, follow the instincts of your "better half" and use them to re-educate your own tendencies. If you are the agreeable partner, you also may have something to learn: high agreeableness often comes with a lack of assertiveness. Here, disagreeable partners can be of help, as their personality frees them from some of the inhibitions that can undermine assertiveness.

6 You walk into the supermarket and an employee doing a promotion jumps out and thrusts a bunch of vouchers into your hand. What's your initial reaction?
a *"Wow – it's my lucky day!"*
b *"What's the catch?"*

7 How do you respond when your partner comes home from work in a bad mood?
a *Avoid doing anything that might set your partner off, and encourage him/her to talk about the problem.*
b *You are on guard about your partner's mood and plan your retaliation if he/she takes it out on you.*

8 Someone at work that you've always vehemently disliked is retiring. During the retirement party you find yourself standing next to this colleague. What would you do?
a *Fire off a parting shot.*
b *Keep quiet – if you've got nothing nice to say, don't say anything.*

Also known as emotional instability, neuroticism describes the tendency to become upset, insecure, emotional, or anxious. Its opposite is emotional stability, or even-temperedness. Along with extroversion/introversion, neuroticism/stability is generally considered to be one of the fundamental big five personality trait dimensions.

Not surprisingly, neuroticism is generally regarded as a negative trait and is associated with negative moods and emotions, such as guilt, shame, and anger. People who score high on this dimension tend to be more prone to anxiety and depression. They are less able to maintain their emotional stability or keep an even temper, and tend to place a negative spin on anything that happens to them. Neurotic people are worriers and defeatists. People who do not score high on this dimension tend to be less self-conscious and more secure.

The diagram on the right shows some of the characteristics, positive and negative, typically associated with neuroticism and its opposite dimension.

The Questionnaire

You and your partner should both complete this quiz and then compare results. Answer as honestly as possible.

1 You've gone on vacation in search of the sun. Once your plane lands, you discover that the weather is wet and windy. What would your immediate reaction be?

a *Typical! The week I'm on vacation there's a storm and no sun!*

b *It'll probably clear up by tomorrow.*

2 The traffic report says there's a rush-hour jam on a major road due to a crash – it's the road that your partner uses to go to work. Would you worry that it might be your partner that crashed?

a *Yes.*

b *No.*

3 You've had a slight disagreement with a work colleague. Would you worry later on that you might have over-reacted, or sleep easy in the knowledge that you were fully justified?

a *Sleep easy.*

b *Worry.*

4 Someone at work notices that you've gotten a haircut and says, "Hey – new haircut!" How would you be most likely to interpret this comment?

a *It means that he/she likes your new haircut.*

b *It means that he/she thinks you have a terrible new look.*

5 How do you normally feel after a test or exam?

a *You did your best; no point worrying about your answers now.*

b *You go over your answers in your head and fret about whether you should have given different ones.*

6 You've taken your partner to meet your parents and your mom proposes bringing out the old album and showing photos of you as a child and teenager. How would you feel?

a *Worried your partner will see what an idiot you looked as a kid.*

b *Sanguine – maybe you look silly, but that was a long time ago.*

7 You're at a party and one of the guests claims he can tell all about your personality just by looking at your palm. What would you be most likely to think?

a *It could be fun.*

b *He might say something unflattering and I'd be embarrassed.*

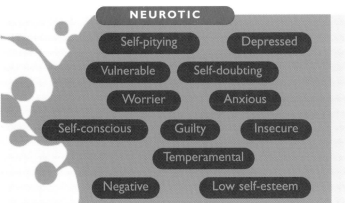

8 If you went on a blind date, do you think that one date would be enough for you to make a good impression, or would it take several dates for the other person to get to know the real you?

a *One date would be enough.*

b *It would take more than one date.*

INTERPRETING THE RESULTS

Use this key to work out your scores and then find the difference between the two. This is your compatibility rating on the neuroticism dimension.

Question/Answer	a	b
1	1	0
2	1	0
3	0	1
4	0	1
5	0	1
6	1	0
7	0	1
8	0	1

(0–2) If you both scored low you are likely to be well-adjusted people who are happy with yourselves, making you good at coping with conflict – essential for long-term relationship health. **(3–6)** You'll have to deal with a fairly normal degree of anxiety and self-doubt. At times you'll have to tread carefully to avoid hurting each other but most of the time you'll be fine. **(7–9)** If you both scored high, you have a joint tendency to be negative and your fragile self-confidence can be shattered easily by a careless word or gesture. This puts your relationship on a shaky footing, as you will have to take special care not to upset each other. On the plus side, you share a similarly bleak outlook on life. **One partner scored high and the other scored low** To some extent the stable partner can compensate for the neurotic one, but over an extended period this can become a burden.

WHAT TO DO ABOUT A MISMATCH

Neuroticism in isolation is a negative and unattractive trait but it is only one dimension of personality. In combination with other traits a degree of neuroticism can be productive and motivating – e.g. in conjunction with conscientiousness it can inspire ambition and hard work. Having said which, there is no doubt that neurotic people have to work harder to maintain relationships over the long-term. If you scored high in neuroticism, pay particular attention to my Plan for Perfect Partnership (see page 152).

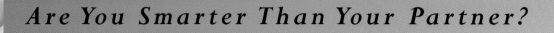
Intelligence tests are controversial because people claim that they are biased against race/class/etc., or that they measure only your ability to do intelligence tests. Some of these objections raise valid points, but a great deal of research shows that intelligence tests are measuring real intelligence and that they are good at doing so.

The following test is based on the General Mental Abilities test devised by Louis Janda et al in 1995, which is used, for example, by some employers to assess prospective employees. It looks at different sub-types of intelligence, including verbal and mathematical, and includes some general knowledge questions (it might seem that these test knowledge rather than intelligence but a) the two are usually related and b) these particular questions also involve some degree of problem solving).

Test 1: Intelligence

This is a multiple-choice test that both you and your partner should complete. You can give yourself a time limit or take as long as you want, so long as you both do it under identical conditions. Score one point for each correct answer.

VERBAL ABILITIES

Select the alternative that best completes the sentence.

1 Exacerbate is to escalate as ascend is to
a *fall*   c *depress*
b *mount*   d *accumulate*

2 Intense is to concentrated as anodyne is to
a *profound*   c *substantial*
b *weighty*   d *banal*

3 Investigate is to accept as prolix is to
a *pithy*   c *meander*
b *drone*   d *stretch*

4 Mobile is to inscrutable as furnish is to
a *bestow*   c *bequeath*
b *eliminate*   d *allow*

5 Bestow is to confer as esoteric is to
a *obvious*   c *occult*
b *plain*   d *transcendent*

6 Antic is to grotesque as mundane is to
a *quotidian*   c *fabulous*
b *unreal*   d *mythic*

GENERAL KNOWLEDGE

7 What is the Celsius equivalent of 0°F?

a *-32°*   c *32°*

b *-17.8°*   d *0°*

8 At which of the following places does water of the same initial temperature come to the boil the most quickly?

a *The Dead Sea.*

b *Times Square.*

c *The top of Mt. Everest.*

d *It takes the same time at all three places.*

9 How many edges does a cube have?

a *12*   c *16*

b *11*   d *10*

10 Which planet has the shortest year?

a *Jupiter*   c *Mars*

b *Venus*   d *Neptune*

11 Which is further north?

a *Oslo*   c *Copenhagen*

b *Reykjavik*   d *Stockholm*

MATHEMATICAL ABILITY

12 If $8x + 4y = 16$, then $2x + y = ?$

a *8*   c *4*

b *½*   d *2*

13 $\frac{2}{5} \times \frac{3}{4} \div \frac{3}{5} =$

a *1/16*   c *18/25*

b *2*   d *½*

14 The bowls club has 60 members. 45 of them are women. What percentage are men?

a *30%*   c *15%*

b *22.5%*   d *25%*

15 Which of the following is the smallest number?

a *16/30*   c *81/160*

b *26/50*   d *32/62*

16 There are 32 players in a tennis tournament where each match is a knockout match. How many matches in the tournament?

a *16*   c *32*

b *31*   d *64*

17 To make up his bags of sweets for trick-or-treaters, Herbie uses 4 toffees for every 6 sherbet lemons. If each bag has 25 sweets in it and the kids get one bag each, how many toffees does each of them get?

a *8*   c *10*

b *9*   d *12*

INTERPRETING THE RESULTS

Match A difference between your scores of 8 points or less.

Mismatch A difference of greater than 8 points. An intelligence mismatch raises a lot of issues. The partner coming second may find the difference adversely affects their self-esteem or that they get frustrated when their partner makes leaps in thought or conversation or doesn't make allowances for them. The more mentally agile partner may also get frustrated and feel unappreciated. Both could become resentful of the other for making them feel bad. All of this depends, however, on how differences in intelligence are perceived. For many couples these simply don't signify compared to more important things such as basic enjoyment of the other's company, how conflicts are resolved, whether each is sensitive to the other's needs, etc.

Test 2: Attitudes to Intelligence

Unless there's a really huge mismatch in IQ, intelligence generally only matters as much as you let it. Use the test below as a quick guide to whether your attitudes to intelligence and intellectuality might cause problems.

In response to the following statements, say whether you think they are true T or false F. Get your partner to do the same.

1 There are few things that bug me more than stupidity.

T   F

2 It irritates me when people use long words.

T   F

3 I think that most of the television news programs have been dumbed down to the point of being unwatchable.

T   F

4 I get frustrated when I have to repeat things because the person I'm talking to is too slow to understand me.

T   F

5 People who scoff at sitcoms on TV are being snobbish.

T   F

6 The people who work in call centers are mostly idiots.

T   F

7 I would rather my kids grew up to be rich than clever.

T   F

8 Sometimes I can't understand why my partner is so slow.

T   F

9 I can't be bothered with science documentaries.

T   F

10 I would rather my children's role models weren't celebrities.

T   F

11 People who do the cryptic crossword are just showing off.

T   F

12 There are few things I dislike more than people who put on airs just because they went to college.

T   F

INTERPRETING THE RESULTS

SCORING

As you've probably noticed there are actually two sets of questions here, so use the scoring key to get your scores on two dimensions – intellectual impatience and intellectual hostility. The former is characterized by the perception that others are being unreasonably or irritatingly slow and that intellectual standards in general are too low, with consequent feelings of superiority. The latter is characterized by feelings of inferiority and hostility to things or people perceived as being intellectual.

Impatience	Hostility
1 **T**	2 **T**
3 **T**	5 **T**
4 **T**	7 **T**
6 **T**	9 **T**
8 **T**	11 **T**
10 **T**	12 **T**

A score of 4 or more in one of the dimensions counts as "high."

Your results in this test need to be interpreted in tandem with the result of Test 1. The following combinations of results are cause for concern:

Test 1 result	Test 2 result	Comments
Mismatch	One partner scored high for Impatience	The "more intelligent" partner may be judgemental and unforgiving; quick to make negative assumptions and responses and insensitive and disrespectful to the "less intelligent" partner.
Mismatch	One partner scored high for Hostility	The "less intelligent" partner may have a chip on his/her shoulder; is likely to feel insecure and act defensively; may make accusations and provoke fights.
Match	One partner scored high for Impatience, the other high for Hostility	Even though both partners are evenly matched for intelligence, they may argue over their responses to the rest of the world, with consequences for everything from viewing and reading habits to choice of friends and how to bring up children.
Mismatch	One partner scored high for Impatience, the other high for Hostility	Partners are likely to fulfil each other's negative predictions and escalate disagreements through mutual defensiveness and hostility. It becomes hard for partners to empathize with one another and treat each other with respect.

WHAT TO DO ABOUT A MISMATCH

The greatest danger from an intellectual mismatch is that partners cease to respect one another. Without respect there is little hope for long-term compatibility and happiness. Maintaining respect is the most important step in overcoming an intellectual mismatch, but you can't simply will this to happen in the face of negative intellectual attitudes. What you need to do first is learn to challenge and adapt those negative attitudes.

NEGATIVE SCHEMA

Negative attitudes such as the impatient and hostile approaches described above are an example of what cognitive psychologists call "negative schema." A negative schema is the mental framework that filters your perceptions, directs the way you analyse those perceptions, and channels the responses that you give as a result. The intellectually impatient person has a mental framework that

makes them perceive as stupid or foolish actions that others might see as natural or harmless, and directs them to respond negatively with impatience or censure where others might be more forgiving and patient.

Changing a negative schema involves first becoming aware that it exists and noticing when it's coming into action. From there you can learn to challenge your negative perceptions and break out of negative patterns of thinking. After all, intelligence only accounts for 20 per cent of your potential business success in life, and it is far better to be emotionally intuitive than have a high IQ if you want to make friends and influence people.

How Emotionally Intelligent Are You?

These days we recognize all kinds of intelligence. We know that violinists have "intelligent" fingers and dancers have "intelligent" feet – all mediated through the brain. Just like computers, some people's brains are configured very differently from others. But besides the abstract skills of reasoning, logic, and problem solving, there is "social intelligence," the ability to understand and relate to people.

In recent years, one component of social intelligence – emotional intelligence (EI) – has come to the fore. Emotional intelligence has been defined as "a type of social intelligence that involves the ability to monitor one's own and others' emotions, to discriminate among them, and to use the information to guide one's thinking and actions." In other words, it's about understanding and working within our network of feelings.

A lot of attention has focused on the role of EI in the workplace, but it's even more central to the field of human relationships. Your level of EI is vital in determining how well you know yourself, understand your partner, communicate your needs and feelings, deal with conflict, and the extent to

Test 1: Emotional Literacy

This questionnaire assesses your abilities in each of these areas so that you can get an overall EI rating to compare with your partner's, together with an idea of how your abilities break down. Rate each of the following statements on a scale of 1 to 5 to show how much you agree or disagree with it, with 1 indicating strong agreement, 3 indicating neither agreement nor disagreement and 5 indicating strong disagreement.

I	2	3	4	5

strongly agree   strongly disagree

1 Seeing other people cry really distresses me.

I	2	3	4	5

2 The opposite sex is a mystery to me.

I	2	3	4	5

3 Back when I was dating I sometimes thought the evening had gone really well only to be given the cold shoulder in the end.

I	2	3	4	5

4 My partner sometimes cries for no reason.

I	2	3	4	5

5 I always know when my friends are upset about something.

I	2	3	4	5

6 My partner gives me looks I just don't understand.

I	2	3	4	5

7 I frequently interrupt my partner when he/she is talking.

I	2	3	4	5

8 Other people rarely "get" my sense of humor.

I	2	3	4	5

9 I wish people would just come out and say "no" when they mean "no."

I	2	3	4	5

10 My friends know they can always talk to me about their problems.

I	2	3	4	5

which you can grow as a person and overcome negative attitudes and patterns of behavior.

EI can be split in several ways, but the main distinction we would draw is between "emotional literacy" and "emotional responsiveness," broadly equivalent to your ability to understand emotions and your ability to deal with them. These are not the same thing. You might very sensitive to emotional nuance, but that doesn't mean you can control the way you respond. Equally, people can be very good at dealing with other people's problems, but be quite lacking in *self*-awareness.

11 **People can be way too sensitive.**

| 1 | 2 | 3 | 4 | 5 |

12 **I wish I knew what my boss wants from me.**

| 1 | 2 | 3 | 4 | 5 |

13 **The breakups I've had in previous relationships have come as a real shock.**

| 1 | 2 | 3 | 4 | 5 |

14 **I can't be expected to know I've upset my partner if he/she won't explain what I've done.**

| 1 | 2 | 3 | 4 | 5 |

15 **I'm not very good at telling jokes.**

| 1 | 2 | 3 | 4 | 5 |

16 **I keep a close eye on the reaction of my colleagues when I'm giving a talk at work.**

| 1 | 2 | 3 | 4 | 5 |

SCORING

The scoring system for this test sounds a little complicated but don't be put off. For each of statements 1, 5, 10, and 16, reverse your score by taking the rating you gave and subtracting it from 6 (if you scored 1 for question 1, subtract this from 6, giving you a score of 5) Do this individually for each of these statements. Once you've done this add the resulting totals to your scores for all the other questions to get a final total.

Test 2: Emotional Responsiveness

Use the same system as test 1 to rate the following statements.

1 What I say is less important than how I say it.

| I | 2 | 3 | 4 | 5 |

2 I can fly off the handle when pushed.

| I | 2 | 3 | 4 | 5 |

3 If someone at work is upset I think it's best to just let them be.

| I | 2 | 3 | 4 | 5 |

4 People ask me for advice but then get upset when they get it.

| I | 2 | 3 | 4 | 5 |

5 Sometimes I make my partner cry or become very angry.

| I | 2 | 3 | 4 | 5 |

6 I have trouble bringing up difficult subjects with my partner.

| I | 2 | 3 | 4 | 5 |

7 My partner knows how I feel about him/her without having to be told.

| I | 2 | 3 | 4 | 5 |

8 If I get dumped by a boy/girlfriend I lose it completely.

| I | 2 | 3 | 4 | 5 |

9 Too much praise makes people bigheaded.

| I | 2 | 3 | 4 | 5 |

10 If I asked for a raise I think I'd get one (assuming I deserved one).

| I | 2 | 3 | 4 | 5 |

11 When it comes to relationships, actions speak louder than words.

| I | 2 | 3 | 4 | 5 |

12 If you're unhappy with something in your relationship you should discuss it at the first possible opportunity.

| I | 2 | 3 | 4 | 5 |

13 After an argument it's best to have a cooling off period for a few days before returning to the subject.

| I | 2 | 3 | 4 | 5 |

14 I have trouble motivating staff who work with or under me.

| I | 2 | 3 | 4 | 5 |

15 After a hard day's work I shouldn't have to deal with my partner's moans about minor issues.

| I | 2 | 3 | 4 | 5 |

16 I get really angry with myself when I make a mistake.

| I | 2 | 3 | 4 | 5 |

SCORING

For statement I you need to reverse your score by taking the rating you gave and subtracting it from 6. Once you've done this add the resulting score to your scores for all the other questions to get a final total.

INTERPRETING THE RESULTS

Add your scores from both tests together to get an overall EI rating, then do the same for your partner.

30–70 Low

71–110 Medium

111–150 High

The first thing to look at is your personal EI rating. With most of the tests in this book your personal score is less important than the relationship between your score and your partner's. In the case of EI, however, a higher score generally increases your compatibility rating whatever your partner's score, because it indicates that you will be better at meeting the emotional challenges of a long-term relationship. People who score lower in EI tests are generally less good at avoiding and/or resolving conflict.

HOW DID YOU COMPARE?

Both scored high A real boost to your long-term compatibility. Your scores suggest that you are both good at sensing each other's moods and responding well to them, and also that you can both express your feelings without losing control of them. Crucially, your chances of working through future conflicts are good because you'll both be able to understand how the other feels and deal with the problem more sensitively.

Both scored low This isn't necessarily a blow to your compatibility. If neither of you are very emotional people then presumably neither of you will mind too much if the other seems distant or unresponsive: your behaviors may match up well even if your feelings remain a mystery to one another. But a lot depends on personal variables. For instance, if one or both of you has low scores on emotional responsiveness, you might be bad at controlling your tempers or have a tendency to over-react. Low scores on emotional literacy can mean that neither partner might sense a brewing storm until it's far too late and the relationship has already suffered irreparable damage.

Both scored medium This is probably the case in the average relationship, but unfortunately statistics tell us that the average relationship is far from perfect. Again, a lot depends on personal

areas of strength and weakness. The stereotypical pattern is that men are from Mars (low EI, particularly in terms of emotional literacy) and women are from Venus (high emotional literacy but perhaps not such good emotional responsiveness) but there are many different permutations, all of which have the potential to lead to misunderstandings and rows.

One partner scored high and the other low In this scenario one partner usually makes the relationship hard work by being uncommunicative or short-tempered, but the other can compensate through greater sensitivity and responsiveness. The danger is that the low EI partner ends up feeling "managed."

One partner scored medium, one low This is the most problematic scenario because one partner is sensitive enough to get hurt but perhaps not emotionally insightful enough to handle it well, while the other may not even be aware of the problems that he/she is causing.

WHAT TO DO ABOUT A MISMATCH

You may not be able to alter EI, but you can learn to work around a low rating. People with poor emotional literacy find it hard to read, understand, and use emotional signals, such as the signs that show a partner is upset. One way to help is to use devices that make these subtle or implicit signals obvious and explicit. Here are two exercises you can use to improve your performance:

• The key-holder: one partner holds a set of keys, a sign that only he/she may speak and that the other person cannot interrupt. Only when the keys are passed over can the other person speak.

• The chair: partners visually demonstrate their mood in relation to a chair. If one partner is speaking and the other moves away from the chair, the first partner knows he/she is upset.

People with poor emotional responsiveness have trouble controlling and expressing their emotions. One way to help this is to cultivate good emotional habits, so that they start to become second nature. For instance, make a point of telling your partner that you love him/her a certain number of times a week; make a routine of counting to ten before replying when having an argument; make an effort to remember special occasions.

Do You Share Creative Minds?

In general terms, creativity is about how imaginative and resourceful you are, but it's a hard characteristic to pin down. The first thing people usually associate with creativity is how artistic or musical a person is, so the first part of this test looks at the ways in which you express your creativity. There's more to a creative mind than drawing, singing, or writing, however, and the second test looks at your creative thinking skills – whether or not you have a creative mind-set and a creative approach to life. (Remember, creativity is a constituent of the openness dimension discussed in Are You Open to New Experiences? on pages 56–7.)

Test 1: Artistic Impulses

For each of the following pursuits commonly associated with creativity, give one rating for your level of interest and one for your level of actual activity in that field. Use a scale of 1–5, where 5 is the highest and 1 indicates little or no interest/activity. Multiply your Interest Rating by your Activity Rating to give an overall score, your IA Rating. Bear in mind that this test is about creative pursuits you enjoy actively – singing, rather than listening to music; writing, rather than reading.

1	2	3	4	5
No interest/activity				High interest/activity

INTERPRETING THE RESULTS

Total up all your IA Ratings to find your TCP Rating and then compare this with your partner's – how big is the difference?

A difference in your TCP Rating of more than 40 counts as a creative mismatch, suggesting that one of you has an artistic bent while the other has little interest in creative pursuits. A difference of more than 70 suggests a real problem, since there is likely to be a clash of priorities over how much of your life each of you devotes to creative pursuits, together with the difference in outlook and attitudes suggested by your differing interests.

Creative pursuit	Interest Rating	Activity Rating	IA Rating
Art (such as painting, drawing, and photography)			
Music (such as playing an instrument, singing, being in a band)			
Writing (such as keeping a diary, storytelling to children, poetry, song writing)			
Decoration (both interior and exterior)			
Crafts and design (such as woodwork, furniture making, embroidery, dressmaking, knitting, model making, flower arranging)			
Landscape and garden design (where horticulture is used for artistic/visual/expressive purposes)			
Body art (such as makeup, nails, hair, tattoos, body piercing)			
Total Creative Pursuits (TCP) Rating			

Test 2: Creative Thinking

Answer and score the following quiz and get your partner to do the same.

1 **When you look at an empty room with bare floorboards and walls stripped back to the plaster, what do you see?**

a *An empty room with bare floorboards and walls stripped back to the plaster.*

b *An opportunity to redecorate.*

c *The room of your dreams with all the colors, fabrics, and furnishings you've always wanted to try out.*

2 **A child asks you a question about rainy weather. You don't know the answer. What do you say?**

a *That you don't know the answer.*

b *That it's something to do with hot and cold air, and you can look it up together when you get home.*

c *That the weather is created by giant dragons with bad head colds who create clouds and rain by sneezing and coughing.*

3 **Your partner has a significant birthday coming up and you want to do something to mark the occasion but don't have much money. What do you do?**

a *Go out — just the two of you — for a nice dinner.*

b *Throw a themed dinner party.*

c *Make a photo/video review of his/her childhood with audio commentary recorded by friends and family.*

4 **Your partner leaves it up to you to organize this year's vacation, and his/her only instruction is to avoid "the same old thing in the same old place." What do you arrange?**

a *The same old thing somewhere new.*

b *A different type of holiday in your usual haunt (such as mountain walking in Greece instead of beach-going in Greece).*

c *Something completely new for both of you.*

5 **What sort of doodles do you draw?**

a *None — doodling's a waste of time, ink, and paper.*

b *Spirals, shapes, flowers, lines, or words.*

c *Pictures, portraits, cartoons, or caricatures.*

6 **You have to do some emergency plumbing to clear the drain, but don't have a plunger. What would you be most likely to do?**

a *Wait until you can get hold of a plunger.*

b *Try and clear the drain some other way.*

c *Fashion a makeshift plunger using half a tennis ball and a broom-handle.*

INTERPRETING THE RESULTS

Score 1 point for each a); 2 for each b); and 3 for each c). How close were your scores? A difference of 8 points or more suggests that you and your partner have very different outlooks on life. A low score indicates you are straight-forward, literal minded, and down to earth; a high score that you are fanciful, imaginative, and resourceful.

WHAT TO DO ABOUT A MISMATCH

• Think about the positive sides. Differing spheres of interest give partners personal space and allow them to bring things back into the relationship, making it stronger.

• Focus on commonality rather than differences. If you feel that common ground is lacking in your relationship, make some! Develop shared interests that suit both your styles.

• When you do look at your differences, ask yourself which are the "deal-breakers" – the differences that you can't live with and that threaten your relationship. These are the issues you must sit down and discuss.

Do You Have a Good Sense of Humor?

GSOH – standing for Good Sense of Humor – is probably the most common acronym in the personal ads section of your newspaper, proof positive of its importance for lonely hearts seeking soulmates. Humor enhances relationships – most obviously it helps partners enjoy one another's company. It also relieves stress, lightens dark moods, and defuses tense situations. Can you and your partner share a joke, or is one of you managing to miss the punch line?

As the Bible tells us, "A merry heart doeth good like a medicine," (Proverbs). Laughter, smiling, and positive moods in general have been shown to relieve stress and affect the body's hormones, neurotransmitters, and immune system directly. For instance, laughter can boost production of endorphins, natural mood-boosting chemicals produced by your brain. This means that sharing a sense of humor, and therefore enjoying a good laugh with, your partner, can boost your sense of well-being. Having someone who finds you funny is also good for your self-esteem.

Perhaps the most crucial role of humor in relationships over the long-term is in coping with crises. Research shows that people who use humor to deal with difficult situations cope much better, with lower levels of stress and depression, than those who don't. In a relationship scenario, partners who are able to retain a sense of humor will come through disagreements and difficulties in much better shape than those who can't. However, a couple must have a matching sense of humor, or jokiness will come off badly.

The Questionnaire

Answer the following questions to build up your own sense of humor compatibility rating.

1 **Write down your three favorite comedy shows and give them Comedy Ratings out of 5. Ask your partner to give his/her own ratings for the shows you've picked. Add up the difference in ratings across the three shows. How do your ratings compare?**

a   *Total difference of 2 or less: Score 1 point.*
b   *Total difference of between 3 and 5: Score 2 points.*
c   *Total difference of 6 or more: Score 3 points.*

2 **Use this scale to say how frequently the following scenarios occur – 1: Very rarely, if ever; 2: Sometimes; 3: Quite often – and then add up your answers.**

a   *You make a joke but your partner takes it the wrong way.*
b   *You find your partner's jokes/witty comments cruel or harsh.*
c   *Your partner can't tell that you're joking about something.*
d   *Your partner uses humor to belittle you or make you feel foolish.*

3 **Compare your partner's behavior while out with friends to his/her behavior when alone with you. Does he/she seem to laugh:**

a   *More with you than with friends: Score 1 point.*
b   *About the same with you as with friends: Score 2 points.*
c   *More with friends than with you: Score 3 points.*

4 **How do you feel about your partner's friends?**

a   *They are a bit dull/straight/worthy: Score 3 points.*
b   *They are funny/amusing to be with: Score 1 point.*
c   *They are a bit boorish/excessive/not as funny as they think they are: Score 3 points.*

5 **Dirty jokes – does your partner find them:**

a   *About as funny as you do: Score 1 point.*
b   *Less acceptable than you: Score 3 points.*
c   *More acceptable than you: Score 3 points.*

INTERPRETING THE RESULTS

How did you score? Add up your score to get your sense of humor compatibility rating. Get your partner to do the same.

8–13 Laughing with one another (Highly compatible)
14–19 Laughing near one another (Intermediate compatibility)
20–24 Laughing at one another (Humor mismatch).
A mismatched sense of humor can reveal the darker side of wit. What one partner thinks is funny another might find acerbic and sarcastic; and that partner might be thought dull and unresponsive in turn.

WHAT TO DO ABOUT A MISMATCH

A sense of humor mismatch often means that partners will need to work harder than the average couple to avoid misunderstandings. Both partners might develop the habit of pausing and thinking before giving knee-jerk responses – either in order to avoid making jokes that might be misinterpreted, or to avoid misinterpreting them. You can compensate for damage done with misunderstood humor by "telegraphing" jokes (for example, preface a potentially sarcastic comment by saying "I mean this as a joke…" or, even better, don't say something that might need such a preface) and by making sure that you express positive regard for your partner more often.

Do You Get Bored With Each Other?

According to decades of research, "sensation seeking," (of which tolerance of boredom is one aspect) is a fundamental and central feature of human personality. More recent research suggests that sensation seeking is a personality dimension that ranks alongside the big five, and appears to show that sensation seeking has a strong genetic component that remains more or less fixed throughout life. This means it's a good idea to find a partner whose sensation-seeking tendencies match your own, since it's not something you can alter to "fit in" with your partner.

A number of different but related components of the sensation-seeking personality can be identified. They include a liking for exciting activities, such as dangerous sports; a liking for new experiences, such as exploring unknown places or meeting eccentric people; a low boredom threshold, which affects how easily you get tired of things and what level of inactivity you can tolerate; and a low level of inhibition, which affects your behavior in social situations and your attitude to social norms and strictures (including laws). The questions below explore all four of these areas.

The Test

For each of the pairs of statements below, choose the one that best describes your preferences. Get your partner to do the same.

1
a When I eat out, I like to try something new every time.
b When I eat out, I like to stick with dishes I know that I like.

2
a I enjoy or would like to try bungee jumping.
b I think anyone who jumps off a bridge is mad.

3
a There's nothing worse than a boring person.
b There's nothing worse than a rude person.

4
a If money was no object I'd go rafting down the Amazon.
b If money was no object I'd stay in the most expensive hotel on the French Riviera.

5
a I like to see my favorite movie again and again.
b I can't watch a movie more than once.

6
a There's nothing wrong with bursting into song on the way home from a night out.
b I don't like to get drunk.

7
a I like to drive fast whenever I can.
b If I got to drive a racing car around a circuit I wouldn't try to reach full speed.

8
a There's nothing wrong with sleeping around in your youth.
b People who have many sexual partners risk catching a sexually transmitted disease.

9
a When I'm on vacation I like to do nothing outside of sunbathing on the beach or by the pool.
b I go crazy after one afternoon sitting around doing nothing.

10
a I love weekends when I have nothing to do and can stay at home reading the papers.
b Weekends allow me to catch up on the culture I don't have time for during the week.

11
a I don't like to swim in deep water – you never know what might swim underneath you.
b I'd love to go scuba diving with sharks.

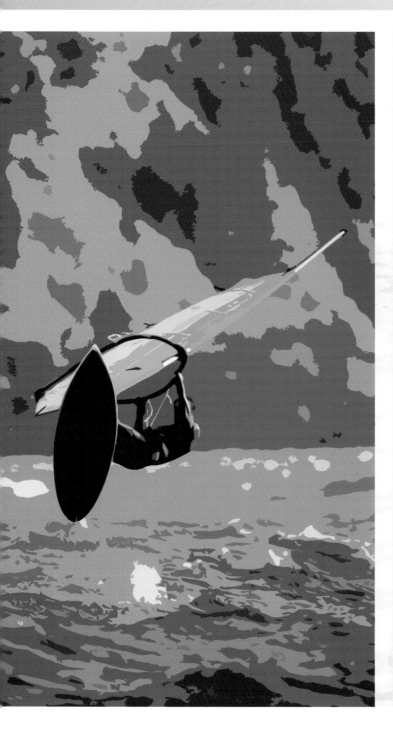

INTERPRETING THE RESULTS

Score one point for each of the following answers:
1: a; 2: a; 3: a; 4: a; 5: b; 6: a; 7:a; 8: a; 9: b; 10: b; 11: b
Compare your score to your partner's. The difference is your boredom threshold compatability rating.

0–3 Match – you and your partner look for similar levels of excitement in your life and have the same capacity to tolerate boredom.

4–11 Mismatch – you and your partner may have a problem. One of you thinks the other is headstrong and excitable, while the other thinks his/her partner is a boring stay-at-home. This could impact on many different aspects of your life, from the relatively trivial, such as deciding where to go on holiday, to the much more weighty, like your attitudes toward sex or how to handle family finances. Even the little things could have big consequences – issues such as what to watch on television, or whether to stay in at all, are what constitute the meat and drink of a relationship. Constant disagreements could lead you to start thinking that you're not, well, compatible.

WHAT TO DO ABOUT A MISMATCH

Research suggests that you are not going to change each other's appetites for adventure and stimulation. One solution is to recognize that each partner has different needs and to allow each other the personal space for your activities/inactivity, but you will need to ensure that your other half doesn't feel hurt or rejected because he/she feels left out.

Compromise may be hard to achieve (you can't do half a bungee jump!), but you could try alternating weekends so that one weekend you decide what you're going to do together, the following weekend it's your partner who decides – and the weekend after that is up for negotiation.

What is Your Happiness Quotient?

One of the fastest growing areas of psychology today is the positive psychology movement, initiated by that "prophet of well-being" Dr. Martin Seligman, of the University of Pennsylvania. This looks at what makes people happy and how life can be made more fulfilling. Among the discoveries of positive psychology is that happiness, although it can be affected by events over the short-term, is a personality characteristic akin to openness or sensation seeking.

You have an individual set level for life satisfaction that is determined by your genes and life experience. Somewhat surprisingly, positive psychology research suggests that the former is more important than the latter. Although your mood may fluctuate around this optimum, its base level is not easily changed. This means that happiness affects your set level like other personality dimensions. If you have a high set level for happiness but your partner doesn't, you may find him/her miserable – your partner, on the other hand, may feel that you have an unrealistic view of life. More generally, most people would prefer a partner who is not temperamentally miserable, so this is a test where individual scores matter as well as relative scores.

The Questionnaire

One of the simplest instruments for measuring happiness is the Personal Well-being Index, designed by Professor Bob Cummins of Deakin University in Australia. All you have to do is give a rating in response to each of the following seven questions using the scale below:

0	1	2	3	4	5	6	7	8	9	10

completely dissatisfied	neutral	completely satisfied

How satisfied are you with:

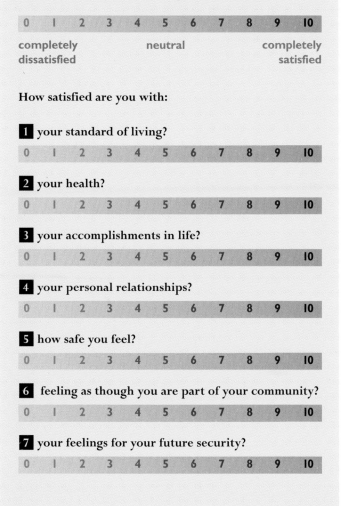

1 your standard of living?

0	1	2	3	4	5	6	7	8	9	10

2 your health?

0	1	2	3	4	5	6	7	8	9	10

3 your accomplishments in life?

0	1	2	3	4	5	6	7	8	9	10

4 your personal relationships?

0	1	2	3	4	5	6	7	8	9	10

5 how safe you feel?

0	1	2	3	4	5	6	7	8	9	10

6 feeling as though you are part of your community?

0	1	2	3	4	5	6	7	8	9	10

7 your feelings for your future security?

0	1	2	3	4	5	6	7	8	9	10

INTERPRETING THE RESULTS

Add up the scores to get your PWI. Get your partner to do the same.

Your PWI is sensitive to recent events, so if something particularly good or bad has happened to you recently, your score may not properly represent your base PWI score. To control for short-term fluctuations, try the test again a few weeks later and take an average of your scores.

A high score for PWI would be between 60–70. The average score is between 35–59. (Scores as low as 35 are within the normal range.) A score of 34 or below indicates a fairly unhappy person. If there is no obvious external cause for the unhappiness then it's probably a matter of temperament. A difference between your scores greater than 17 is more than average and might indicate a happiness mismatch.

WHAT TO DO ABOUT A MISMATCH

If you and your partner seem to have differing levels of cheerfulness there may be a reason for it. Compare notes on the next test, which looks at your life history and its major events, and may reveal sources of long-term unhappiness. This could explain your differences. Boosting your personal happiness set level may be more difficult, but Dr. Seligman, who coined the phrase "positive psychology," says that if you identify your personal strengths and work to those, you can discover more meaning in your life and become happier.

Your life history is the sum of the events that have happened over the whole of your life, and it affects your entire psychology, including your current state of mind, your coping ability, and your long-term outlook on life. This makes it an important influence on compatibility. If you and your partner share similar life histories in terms of major life events, you are likely to have matching outlooks on life and equivalent stores of experience, with all that this entails.

The following test is a modified version of one devised by psychologists Holmes and Rahe in 1967. They drew up a table that assigned points values to different life events, showing how much of an impact each one had – ranging from the loss of a child or spouse at the top of the table, to minor changes in sleeping habits at the bottom. They wanted to look at life events in a quantitative way, with a system that effectively said moving house (27 points) + getting divorced (73 points) = death of a spouse (100 points). This makes sense if you're using the values to assess something with no associated value judgments, such as stress level. For our purposes, however, we need a system that assesses life events on a qualitative basis, acknowledging that different life experiences are qualitatively different – that only someone who has lost a member of his/her immediate family can understand what it's like for another person in the same situation. So, in my version of the table, life events are put into categories rather than assigned points. It's not a perfect system, but it does provide a rough way to make life histories comparable in a simple fashion.

The Test

This table lists major life events and assigns them to categories.
You can add more life events – but not more categories.

Category A	Category B	Category C	Category D
Death of a child	Divorce	Severe injury	Loss of job
Death of a spouse	Loss of close family member/ parent after age 16	Victim of assault	Infidelity on your part
Loss of a parent before age 16	Imprisonment	Chronic or congenital medical condition	Severe accident (but without severe injury)
Victim of abuse or rape	Life-threatening or severely debilitating condition, illness, or injury	Bankruptcy	Trouble with the law
	Alcoholism or other type of dependency	Loss of home through accident or repossession	Sexual dysfunction
		Death of close friend	Financial problems
		Children (having one or more)	Large mortgage
		Separation	Victim of crime (such as burglary)
		Spousal infidelity	World travel
			Higher education

INTERPRETING THE RESULTS

For each category, compare how many "hits" you got with those of your partner. Matching life histories can be a big plus for your likely relationship compatibility, particularly if you share significant events from categories A or B. If you have suffered something like this it may have proved a barrier to past relationships. But a category A or B match may actually enhance your compatibility because you share an understanding of coping with a difficult life event.

Mismatch scenarios:
Category A Applies to one partner only.
Category B Applies to one partner only or a difference of 2 "hits" or more.
Category C A difference of 2 "hits" or more.
Category D A difference of 4 "hits" or more.

WHAT TO DO ABOUT A MISMATCH

Mismatching life histories can place a barrier between the most committed and/or otherwise well-matched partners because one partner has life experience that the other cannot understand, no matter how much he/she tries. Potential consequences include partners feeling shut off from one another and genuine failure to grasp each other's motivations, fears, needs, and feelings. Overcoming these barriers requires serious emotional investment, trust, and sensitivity on both sides. A good starting point is for each partner to acknowledge the others' experiences.

Your childhood experiences have a major impact on your present-day approach to life, including your approach to relationships and your chances of getting along with a partner. One vital clue to compatibility is whether or not you share one of the most fundamental aspects of childhood: what order you were born into your family.

The most important influence on your childhood was your family, and your place in the family was determined by your birth order – whether you were a first-born, middle, youngest, or only child, and whether you were a girl with several brothers or a boy with lots of sisters.

The importance of birth order to the family environment and therefore to how someone's personality develops was first described by the Austrian psychoanalyst Alfred Adler. He realized that a first-born child develops a special relationship with his or her parents, and that the arrival of subsequent children changes this relationship and creates a new style of interaction between the siblings. Your place in the birth order, and thus how you relate to your siblings, can often be matched to your style of emotional relating for the rest of your life.

Birth Order Assessment

See if your personality matches the following descriptions, and get your partner to do the same. If your birth orders don't match, ask yourselves whether the influence of your place in the family has given you characteristics that complement or antagonize your mutual behavior.

FIRST BORN
You tend to be serious, conscientious, perfectionist, and a high-achiever. As the eldest, you often bore the weight of your parents' expectations. You were expected to behave better than the other children and had more responsibility placed on your shoulders. In adult life, you can suffer from taking on too much, being over-cautious, and not really taking into account your own needs.

MIDDLE BORN
You tend to have a complex mix of sometimes contradictory characteristics – you are a mediator who dislikes conflict, independent but fiercely loyal to your friends. You may be either easy-going or impatient. Middle children often feel under-appreciated or left out. In adult life, you can be good at negotiating and compromise but may also lack assertiveness or feel bitter that you are not given enough attention.

LAST BORN
You tend to be charming, affectionate, and outgoing but may also be manipulative, spoiled, impatient, and wayward! As the baby of the family, a last-born child can be spoiled but also feel disempowered. In later life you may duck responsibility and expect to get away with more than you should, and you are more likely to live an "irregular" lifestyle.

ONLY CHILDREN

You are generally considered to have a mix of first- and last-born characteristics. Like a first born, you carried the weight of parental expectation, but like a last-born you got all the attention and may have been spoiled. In adulthood you may become a perfectionist and find it hard to get on with contemporaries, and you may need to lighten up and expect just a bit less of yourself.

SPECIAL CASES

Siblings born more than five years apart may not occupy the same roles in relationship to one another, while gender influences can be of great importance. Children tend to identify more with same-sex parents and siblings, while solitary boys in a group of girls have their own issues, and vice versa.

INTERPRETING THE RESULTS

Match If you and your partner share the same place in your respective birth orders then you instantly have a huge childhood influence in common. Only someone with the same birth order can properly understand the circumstances and strains to which you were exposed when you were growing up.

Mismatch In this situation, there may be things about one another that you won't intuitively understand. On the other hand, each type of birth order personality has its demands, strengths, and weaknesses, and it may require a slightly different personality to complement these. If your partner is an only child, for instance, but you are a last born, your tendency to be easy-going may be just what your perfectionist partner needs.

WHAT TO DO ABOUT A MISMATCH

Birth order is prime in framing personality. The personality types described are very generalized, easily altered by spacing and gender, and by no means cut-and-dry, so it's your actual personality that matters, not simply your place in a sequence.

Obviously, you can't change your birth order, but you can talk about aspects of each other's personality that grate, and work on overcoming them or compromising your way around them. This can help you to break out of entrenched views and accept that because your partner has had a different experience of life from you, he or she has different reactions to you. Put yourself in your partner's proverbial shoes and empathize with his or her view of the world and of your relationship in particular. Writing down your thoughts can help, and also gives the exercise more meaning.

The Family Atmosphere Test

A major factor in childhood development is parenting style – the atmosphere created by your parents in terms of their expectations and the ways in which they disciplined and rewarded you. Through their parenting styles, parents provide children with models of how to behave in order to win attention and affection. Most of us would like to think that we no longer live our lives in an attempt to please or gain attention from our parents, but as children we absorbed and internalized these models of behavior. To a large extent they will always be with us, guiding and motivating much of our behavior. This has obvious ramifications for your search for love, because the partner who suits you best will be one whose emotional style matches your own.

The Family Atmosphere test uses a mini-inventory of questions relating to family background and parenting style to assess what sort of family environment you grew up in and whether it matches up with that of your partner. The test discriminates between three categories that can be used to describe family atmosphere:

- loud, expressive, dramatic, *vs* quiet, sensible, reserved
- close, affectionate, involved *vs* distant, cold
- strict *vs* relaxed.

The Test

The following test consists of 15 statements referring to your parents (or parent, if you were primarily brought up by one parent only) and your family environment when you were growing up. Go through the test with your partner. For each item, each of you should choose an answer and see whether your choices agree. For each question on which you don't agree, score one point.

1   a   There were often people around at your house.
     b   Your parents hardly ever had guests.

2   a   You ate family meals together around the table.
     b   You ate family meals together in front of the TV.
     c   You didn't eat together much.

3   a   Your parents never drank much when the kids were around.
     b   Your parents were happy to "let their hair down" in front of you.

4   a   Your family used to play lots of games together.
     b   Games were something for the kids to do.

5   a   Your parents used to kiss and hug a lot.
     b   Your parents rarely displayed much affection.

6   a   If you went to a party and you got back later than the time agreed with your parents, they would hit the roof and you'd be in hot water.
     b   If you went to a party and you got back later than the time agreed with your parents, it wasn't the end of the world.
     c   You were allowed to come back whenever you wanted.

7
a Your parents used to have fights that the whole family could hear.
b If your parents argued they kept it under wraps.

8
a When you had friends over your parents would keep a close eye on what you were up to.
b When you had friends over you were allowed to go off on your own and do whatever you wanted to.

9
a Grandparents, aunts, uncles, and cousins frequently visited – or you often were at their houses.
b You hardly ever saw your extended family.

10
a Family holidays used to involve everyone joining in (setting up camp, playing on the beach).
b Holidays were a chance for your parents to take a bit of a break from child-minding duties.

11
a If your parents had caught you smoking they would have screamed and shouted at you and grounded you for months.
b If your parents had caught you smoking they would have given you a big lecture on the evils of smoking and made you promise never to do it again.
c If your parents had caught you smoking they wouldn't have cared too much.

12
a Your parents used to kiss and hug you a lot.
b Your parents were quite reserved with you.

13
a Your parent of the same gender had a private room (a study or dressing room) where you weren't welcome.
b Your parent of the same gender used to love sharing his/her private room with you.

14
a The kitchen was the center of the household.
b The living room was the center of the household.
c No one particular room was the obvious center of the household.

15
a Your family was voluble, excitable, and raucous.
b Your family was quiet, careful, and restrained most of the time.

INTERPRETING THE RESULTS

How did you score?

0–4 Matching family atmospheres – should give you plenty of common ground on which to forge a deep and instinctive bond. The only danger is that if you both have bad emotional habits that date back to your upbringing, you will not temper each other's excesses.

5–10 Some areas of mismatch – look carefully at the questions you answered differently and think how these aspects of your upbringing have affected your emotional styles today. In identifying the roots of your emotional style you may also gain important insights into the roots of the differences between you and your partner.

11–15 Mismatch – lacking common ground in your past may make it harder to find in the future.

WHAT TO DO ABOUT A MISMATCH

Consider that you might be complementary rather than similar, and use your strengths to help compensate for each other's areas of emotional difficulty. For example, if you come from a loud, dramatic family and have trouble engaging in a discussion without turning it into a shouting match, but your partner had a more reserved, level-headed background, follow his/her lead when it comes to talking over difficult topics.

Do You Have Similar Tastes?

How does your personality manifest itself in everyday life? One of the most obvious ways is through your likes and dislikes – the way you feel about the little things in life. A lot of these personal preferences might seem trivial, especially when considered in the arena of "big issues" such as compatibility, but these are the day-to-day things that may help or harm your life together.

Couples forge and strengthen their pair bond through sharing experiences and thereby generating shared histories. The things you do together make up the content of your "shared story," and a lot of being a couple is the presentation of that story to the world. All of this is only possible if you enjoy doing things together, and this depends on your likes and dislikes – the more trivial they seem the more important they may be. Take your taste in TV programs. This may seem inconsequential, but surveys show that the most common joint activity for couples is watching TV. Mismatching ideas about what to watch could lead to more than just battles for command of the remote.

The Test

There's nothing very scientific about this test, although it does try to account for some of the vagaries of taste by getting you to make an average rating for each category. Basically, the chart is fairly self-explanatory – you record your top three favorites under each category and then your partner gives each choice a rating out of 10. You then average the three ratings (by adding them together and dividing by 3) to get an average rating for each category, and total up all of the averages across all 10 of the categories. Then you do the same for your partner's choices.

TV PROGRAMS	
Your top three	Partner's rating
1	☐
2	☐
3	☐
Average:	☐

Your partner's top three	Your rating
1	☐
2	☐
3	☐
Average:	☐

FOODS	
Your top three	Partner's rating
1	☐
2	☐
3	☐
Average:	☐

Your partner's top three	Your rating
1	☐
2	☐
3	☐
Average:	☐

FILMS

Your top three	Partner's rating
1	☐
2	☐
3	☐
	Average: ☐

Your partner's top three	Your rating
1	☐
2	☐
3	☐
	Average: ☐

WORLD LEADERS

Your top three	Partner's rating
1	☐
2	☐
3	☐
	Average: ☐

Your partner's top three	Your rating
1	☐
2	☐
3	☐
	Average: ☐

MUSICAL ARTISTS

Your top three	Partner's rating
1	☐
2	☐
3	☐
	Average: ☐

Your partner's top three	Your rating
1	☐
2	☐
3	☐
	Average: ☐

INTERIOR DECORATION STYLES

Your top three	Partner's rating
1	☐
2	☐
3	☐
	Average: ☐

Your partner's top three	Your rating
1	☐
2	☐
3	☐
	Average: ☐

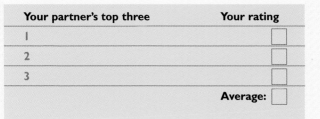

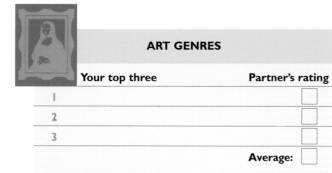

ART GENRES

Your top three	Partner's rating
1	☐
2	☐
3	☐
	Average: ☐

Your partner's top three	Your rating
1	☐
2	☐
3	☐
	Average: ☐

SPORTS

Your top three	Partner's rating
1	☐
2	☐
3	☐
	Average: ☐

Your partner's top three	Your rating
1	☐
2	☐
3	☐
	Average: ☐

TV PERSONALITIES

Your top three	Partner's rating
1	☐
2	☐
3	☐
	Average: ☐

Your partner's top three	Your rating
1	☐
2	☐
3	☐
	Average: ☐

BOOKS

Your top three	Partner's rating
1	☐
2	☐
3	☐
	Average: ☐

Your partner's top three	Your rating
1	☐
2	☐
3	☐
	Average: ☐

Your total: ☐   Your partner's total: ☐

INTERPRETING THE RESULTS

Plot your results on the graph, using your total as the X axis and your partner's as the Y. Draw a straight rule from both your scores. In which band do your scores meet?

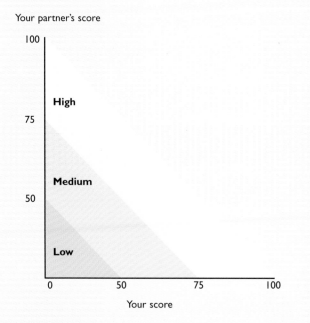

Your partner's score

Your score

CATEGORIES

Low compatibility You and your partner are like chalk and cheese! Staying in can't be much fun because you can't agree which program to watch or what music to listen to, but going out is no good either because you can't agree what movie to see or in which restaurant to eat.

Medium compatibility Some of your partner's favorite things leave you cold, and vice versa, but there's plenty of common ground here with which to work.

High compatibility You are like two peas in a pod! The only danger is that if you both like doing exactly the same things, you could end up spending every minute together.

WHAT TO DO ABOUT A MISMATCH

If you and your partner can't agree on the little things in life then you must ask yourselves how you feel about the big things. Take a look at the beliefs test (pages 108–9), and the money (pages 110–11), career (pages 112–13), and life plan (pages 116–17) tests, to see how compatible you are when it comes to more important issues. If you match up well on these, your poor score on this test suggests that you are compatible deep down but are complementary rather than similar when it comes to day-to-day life. This can be a strength, offering you a relationship that challenges you and is therefore unlikely to get stuck in a rut.

On a more practical level, overcome your mismatch by searching hard for things that you do both like – there may be more than you think. If all else fails, try using the 7-day plan, where each partner has the "power" on certain days of the week. By adopting a formal arrangement like this you can avoid damaging power struggles that undermine your relationship. You might even learn to like each other's favorite television shows.

After years of talking to, recording, and analyzing exchanges between partners, one American expert on couples in conflict claims to have found a simple but effective method for assessing long-term compatibility and predicting future relationship success.

This research looks at the ratio of praise to blame in a couple's exchanges – simply put, the number of positive things a couple say to each other versus the number of negative things. The higher the ratio – the more positive things that are said – the higher the couple's chances of staying together. And it is claimed that the praise:blame (P:B) ratio can be used to predict whether a couple will still be together in five years with a 90 per cent success!

So how does it work? A low P:B ratio doesn't necessarily mean that partners don't like one another, but that they've gotten into the habit of seeing each other in a negative light. In psychological terms, they've developed a negative schema for viewing their partners. Once this pattern has developed, it can be hard to break, with the result that partners lose sight of what brought them together, fail to deal constructively with difficulties that may arise, and eventually become unable to sustain the relationship.

The Questionnaire

Ideally, this questionnaire should be done by an impartial observer, who can look at a transcript of a conversation between people whose names and genders are anonymous to him/her, and make relatively objective assessments of statements in order to categorize them as positive or negative. In practice, you're not likely to find a suitable volunteer for this role , so we'll have to make do with looking at the kinds of responses you and your partner give to one another. Try to answer the questions as honestly as possible, picking the one that most resembles the answer you would give rather than the answer you think you ought to give.

1 Your partner has offered to do the cooking but seems to be causing chaos in the kitchen. How would you most likely react?

a *Keep quiet, because if you haven't got anything nice to say you shouldn't say anything.*

b *Offer constructive advice and criticism.*

2 You've just spent a considerable sum of (non-refundable) money on a coat your partner's seen on sale at half the usual price. How would he/she most likely react?

a *Ask you to be a bit more careful and look around to check for lower prices in the future.*

b *Compliment you on your new coat.*

3 You've come third in a competition at the local fair. What would your partner be most likely to say?

a *Well done!*

b *How come you didn't win?*

4 You and your partner have just been to see a movie. Your partner says that he/she loved every minute of it and really related to the lead character on a personal level. You hated it. When he/she asks you what you thought, what would you be most likely to say?

a *Admit that you didn't like it.*

b *Say how much you liked the lead character.*

5 The pair of you are on your way to your partner's office Christmas party. At the same event last year your partner embarrassed you both, and makes a sheepish joke about it. How would you be most likely to respond?

a   *Laugh along with the joke.*

b   *Ask him/her not to embarrass you again.*

6 Your partner is driving and you're supposed to be navigating. You come to a turnoff but don't know if you're supposed to be taking it. How would your partner most likely respond?

a   *Snap at you.*

b   *Tell you it doesn't matter as he/she can always drive on to the next exit and turn round.*

INTERPRETING THE RESULTS

Calculate how many P(raise) answers you got and how many B(lame) answers you got using this scoring table:

Question/Answer	P	B
1	a	b
2	b	a
3	a	b
4	b	a
5	a	b
6	b	a

Now divide the number of Ps you got by the number of Bs. This is your P:B ratio.

According to the research mentioned earlier, if your P:B ratio is 5 or more then you are highly compatible. If it is 2 or less, then you may be mismatched. If your figure fell somewhere in between, you have a lot of work to do.

WHAT TO DO ABOUT A MISMATCH

The P:B ratio is all about respect. Partners who respect one another will restrict their negative comments to each other even if they are upset about something. Partners whose exchanges are negative are displaying a lack of respect.
To break out of the habit of negative exchanges you need to:

• Train yourself to realize you're doing it.

• Deal properly with issues that are giving you a negative view of your relationship.

• Learn to see your partner in a more positive light again.

What's Your Arguing Style?

Even the most compatible partners have arguments, and over the course of a long-term relationship you can expect to have innumerable fights, big and small. Sometimes, arguments are actually necessary and useful, but too many negative exchanges in relation to positive ones is a symptom of poor relationship health. How you argue is also relevant.

When "successful" couples argue, they maintain respect and sensitivity for one another while managing to have a constructive argument that doesn't resort to personal attacks, exaggerations, or ultimatums. They may not necessarily solve problems or reach happy compromises, but they do manage to clear the air, reassure each other that both sides have been heard, and move on. "Unsuccessful" couples are those who either fail to hold difficult but necessary arguments, or who argue in a destructive rather than constructive manner. Which sort are you?

The Test

This test looks at argumentativeness as a personality dimension and compares your arguing style with your partner's. Rate the following statements as:

1 Doesn't describe me at all
3 Could be true, depending on circumstances
5 Describes me perfectly

1 I'll pick an argument wherever and whenever I can.

| 1 | 2 | 3 | 4 | 5 |

2 It's more important to avoid an argument than to be right.

| 1 | 2 | 3 | 4 | 5 |

3 I would never back down from an argument.

| 1 | 2 | 3 | 4 | 5 |

4 I think challenging debate makes for good mental discipline.

| 1 | 2 | 3 | 4 | 5 |

5 I will often agree with someone to avoid an argument.

| 1 | 2 | 3 | 4 | 5 |

6 I think a fight can clear the air.

| 1 | 2 | 3 | 4 | 5 |

7 I hate it when I can see there's an argument coming.

| 1 | 2 | 3 | 4 | 5 |

8 I can give as good as I get.

| 1 | 2 | 3 | 4 | 5 |

9 Whenever I get in a fight I always vow that it's the last time.

| 1 | 2 | 3 | 4 | 5 |

10 I enjoy the intellectual challenge of a good debate.

| 1 | 2 | 3 | 4 | 5 |

11 I hate to lose my temper.

| 1 | 2 | 3 | 4 | 5 |

12 I prefer to avoid argumentative people whenever possible.

| 1 | 2 | 3 | 4 | 5 |

13 You should never avoid an issue just because it's controversial.

| 1 | 2 | 3 | 4 | 5 |

14 I'm happy if I can foresee and head off a fight.

| 1 | 2 | 3 | 4 | 5 |

INTERPRETING THE RESULTS

SCORING

A Add up your scores for statements 1, 3, 4, 6, 8, 10, and 13.
B Separately, add up your scores for statements 2, 5, 7, 9, 11, 12, and 14.

Subtract total B from A to get your overall argumentativeness score – the maximum possible is +28 while the minimum possible is -28. A high score indicates that you are highly argumentative and not only don't mind, but actively seek out, arguments. A low score suggests that you are avoidant when it comes to conflict.

Get your partner to calculate his/her score and plot your respective overall scores on the scale below.

Which area of the scale did your combined plot put you in?
Yellow (0 to +/-7) This is the most promising in terms of future relationship success – couples in this region are likely to air problems when necessary, but avoid excessive conflict.
Red (+21 to +28) Where both partners score high on the argumentative dimension the forecast is stormy, with a high chance of rows. As we saw in the last test, this can be bad news.
Blue (-21 to -28) Where both partners score in the avoidant end of the argumentativeness spectrum, the relationship is like a boat sailing on smooth but iceberg-infested waters. Important issues don't go away just because they aren't dealt with – they could resurface later and scupper your partnership.

Orange/Green (+7 to +21/-7 to -21) A mismatch here could be the worst of both worlds – one partner habitually reacts in exactly the way calculated to most upset the other. The argumentative partner may get frustrated that issues aren't dealt with, while the avoidant partner may feel browbeaten or nagged.

WHAT TO DO ABOUT A MISMATCH

If you can learn to adopt the right style of argument – able to use listening and summarizing skills, synthesize points, and negotiate sensibly – you can safely negotiate even the mismatch scenarios.

Problem styles for high argumentativeness include:
- AGGRESSIVE – browbeating; domineering; mistakes aggression for assertiveness.
- ARGUING FOR THE SAKE OF IT – likes a good argument; consistently oppositional.
- PARANOID – irrational; delusional; goes over-the-top.

Problem styles for high avoidance include:
- FLUSTERED – words come out in wrong order; the opening mouth before engaging brain phenomenon.
- PLACATORY – agrees to anything for the sake of keeping the peace.

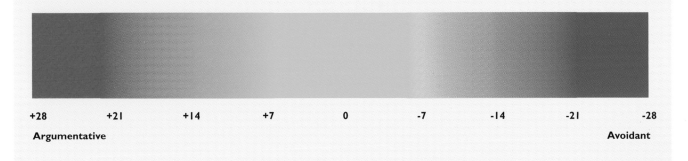

| +28 | +21 | +14 | +7 | 0 | -7 | -14 | -21 | -28 |

Argumentative   **Avoidant**

What is Your Love Profile?

A number of psychological theories have been put forward to describe love. Of these theories, the most popular – the one that most resonates with people's own experience of love – is probably Robert Sternberg's triangular theory. Sternberg identifies three main components of love, and says that different forms of love reflect different combinations of these components. The three components are passion, intimacy, and commitment.

- Passion: This is the component that is strongest at the start of a romantic relationship. It includes sexual excitement and attraction ("chemistry"), and euphoric romantic feelings.
- Intimacy: This component develops in the second stage of a relationship as partners open up to one another and share their thoughts, feelings, needs, and fears. Intimacy is about feeling close to and secure with your partner.
- Commitment: This is the component that develops as a relationship becomes mature. Commitment is about feeling loyal to your partner and to your relationship; it's about stability, security, and belonging.

The Test

Rate each of the statements below on a score of 1 to 10, with 1 being "Disagree," 5 being "Moderately agree," and 10 being "Very strongly agree."

1	2	3	4	5	6	7	8	9	10

Disagree — Moderately agree — Very strongly agree

PASSION

1 You idealize your partner.

1	2	3	4	5	6	7	8	9	10

2 You feel excited just thinking about your partner.

1	2	3	4	5	6	7	8	9	10

3 You find your partner very sexy.

1	2	3	4	5	6	7	8	9	10

4 Your partner turns you on.

1	2	3	4	5	6	7	8	9	10

5 You can't stop thinking about your partner.

1	2	3	4	5	6	7	8	9	10

6 You adore your partner.

1	2	3	4	5	6	7	8	9	10

7 Love songs and romantic movies make you think of your partner.

1	2	3	4	5	6	7	8	9	10

8 You can't keep your hands off each other.

1	2	3	4	5	6	7	8	9	10

INTIMACY

1 Your partner really understands you.

| 1 | 2 | 3 | 4 | 5 | 6 | 7 | 8 | 9 | 10 |

2 You really understand your partner.

| 1 | 2 | 3 | 4 | 5 | 6 | 7 | 8 | 9 | 10 |

3 You trust your partner.

| 1 | 2 | 3 | 4 | 5 | 6 | 7 | 8 | 9 | 10 |

4 You and your partner talk about everything.

| 1 | 2 | 3 | 4 | 5 | 6 | 7 | 8 | 9 | 10 |

5 You've told your partner all about your greatest fears and dreams.

| 1 | 2 | 3 | 4 | 5 | 6 | 7 | 8 | 9 | 10 |

6 You're close to your partner.

| 1 | 2 | 3 | 4 | 5 | 6 | 7 | 8 | 9 | 10 |

7 Your partner can count on you.

| 1 | 2 | 3 | 4 | 5 | 6 | 7 | 8 | 9 | 10 |

8 Your partner is emotionally supportive.

| 1 | 2 | 3 | 4 | 5 | 6 | 7 | 8 | 9 | 10 |

COMMITMENT

1 You worry about your partner's health.

| 1 | 2 | 3 | 4 | 5 | 6 | 7 | 8 | 9 | 10 |

2 You are responsible for your partner.

| 1 | 2 | 3 | 4 | 5. | 6 | 7 | 8 | 9 | 10 |

3 You're in it for the long-term.

| 1 | 2 | 3 | 4 | 5 | 6 | 7 | 8 | 9 | 10 |

4 If things got difficult, you'd still feel committed.

| 1 | 2 | 3 | 4 | 5 | 6 | 7 | 8 | 9 | 10 |

5 You can't imagine splitting up.

| 1 | 2 | 3 | 4 | 5 | 6 | 7 | 8 | 9 | 10 |

6 Your relationship is solid.

| 1 | 2 | 3 | 4 | 5 | 6 | 7 | 8 | 9 | 10 |

7 No one could come between you.

| 1 | 2 | 3 | 4 | 5 | 6 | 7 | 8 | 9 | 10 |

8 You'll always feel responsible for your partner.

| 1 | 2 | 3 | 4 | 5 | 6 | 7 | 8 | 9 | 10 |

DRAWING UP YOUR TRIANGLE

Add up your scores for each component and use them to plot positions along the three axes of this graph.

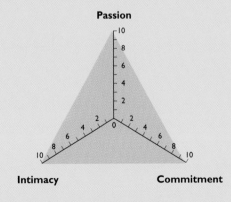

Now use the three points to draw a triangle.

INTERPRETING THE RESULTS

What do your scores reveal? What shape is your triangle? Is it slewed along one axis? Is most of its area between two of the axes? Or is it an equilateral triangle (one where the angles made by all three corners are the same)? As Robert Sternberg explains, there are eight possible ways to combine the three components of love, giving eight types of feeling. This table tells you how to interpret your triangle. Count any score above 40 on any of the three components as "high," and any score below 40 as "low," then do the same for your partner's triangle.

Passion score	Intimacy score	Commitment score	Triangle shape	Category
Low	Low	Low	Tiny	1
High	Low	Low	Skewed toward top	2
Low	High	Low	Skewed toward bottom left	3
Low	Low	High	Skewed toward bottom right	4
High	High	Low	Most of triangle is toward the left	5
Low	High	High	Most of triangle is toward the bottom	6
High	Low	High	Most of triangle is toward the right	7
High	High	High	Equilateral triangle	8

If you find that your scores fall at the midway point of one or more of the axes, and that your triangle doesn't quite fit the shapes described here but falls between two categories, it may be that your feelings for your partner combine elements of both. Read both descriptions and use them to inform your thinking about your relationship. Which is your category?

1 Non-love Low scores for all three components. Non-love describes the relationship we have with companions, friends, or passing acquaintances. It also might describe a relationship that has endured many different stages and phases and has emerged as an independent one, loosely held together.

2 Infatuation Only passion is high. This often describes the initial stage of a relationship, before the other two components have had time to develop, but it's not sustainable in the long-term.

3 Liking Only intimacy is high. Liking is how we feel toward friends – we can be close to them but don't feel romantic or sexual toward them. Nevertheless, we may feel comfortable living with them and may be prepared to manage with less passion than we had previously expected.

4 Empty love Only commitment is high. Common in long-term relationships that have run out of steam. Partners may feel that they should stick together for the sake of the kids but they no longer click emotionally or physically. However, the value of a shared past counts.

5 Romantic love Both passion and intimacy are high, but commitment is low. This type of love is common in second-stage relationships, where partners are really "into" one another but maybe haven't had time to develop commitment.

6 Companionable love Intimacy and commitment are high, but passion is low. Describes relationships where the passion has died but there is still warmth, affection, and a desire to make a life together. Common in long-term couples.

7 Fatuous love Passion and commitment are high but intimacy is low. Describes couples who have fallen head over heels for each other and gotten married, but then find out that they don't have much in common and may not even like each other much – or maybe they just haven't had time to develop intimacy.

8 Consummate love All three components are high. This is the ideal to which to aspire – it normally describes successful long-term couples who love and need each other and also retain a spark in the bedroom. The trick is to make this type of love last.

Which type are you? Bearing in mind that no relationship is ideal, however much you want it to be, don't be disconcerted if your particular type of love falls short. In fact, you can comfort yourself with the knowledge that this is normal. In addition, the scores you award yourself may reflect your current state of mind. And that can change. Since you may feel different in a day, week, or month, take the test again at a later stage. There is also a possibility that your test results may be describing a phase – a stage in a progression toward consummate love. Intimacy and commitment both need time to develop. Regaining lost passion is a trickier issue, but it is possible to put the zing back into your sex life if you are both committed.

HOW DO YOU COMPARE WITH YOUR PARTNER?
A good test of compatibility is to compare your triangle of love with your partner's. Sternberg says that compatible couples will have similarly shaped triangles, showing that you both have the same picture of your relationship – this is called congruency. If your triangles don't match up, see what the differences are and work on them.

PART FOUR

Are You Economically and Socially Compatible?

Today we marry for love – hopefully our partner will be the man or woman of our dreams. Ah, romance! This is the way we do things in the western world, and yet not so long ago marriage was an arranged process in every society. Rising rates of divorce in the west now pose this controversial question – have we let ideals of love and romance blind us to the reality of what really makes relationships work?

The principal change over the past 100 years has been to choose romantic love as the preeminent factor far above more pragmatic issues of class, wealth, and "suitability." We worship at the shrine of desire. Today, in the West, we ask "Are they in love?" and not "Are they a good match?"

The triumph of love

The roots of this process can be traced as far back as the medieval idea of courtly love, which in many ways flowered into the early nineteenth-century notion of romantic love. But it's only as a result of the huge social and economic revolutions of the twentieth century (eroding class barriers, spreading wealth, and speeding social mobility) that our partnering priorities have changed significantly.

Nowadays, we take the fruits of this transformation for granted and often forget how modern the idea of "marriage-for-love" actually is. Even as recently as 1967, three-quarters of female US college students questioned in a survey said they would marry someone they didn't love if they thought it would bring them economic benefit. In the twenty-first century, less than thirty years later, attitudes like this are seen as unacceptably old-fashioned. It's currently considered cold and cynical to rate social and economic variables above interpersonal ones.

The bottom line

But was there, perhaps, a touch of wisdom in the older methods of mate selection? Maybe the harder-nosed approach of a few generations ago was preferable to the fallibilities of unlimited choice? Statistics certainly suggest as much. Even today, and despite all our talk of love, the attraction of opposites and the adoption of multi-cultural ideals, the vast majority of successful relationships are between people of overwhelmingly similar or near-similar backgrounds.

Whether we approve or not, socio-economic factors also determine whether we will be happy in our choice of partners. Couples who share similar backgrounds, aspirations, attitudes, and opinions on key socio-economic issues such as class, ethnicity, earning potential, and career goals are more likely to enjoy long-term relationship happiness than those who don't.

What's in this section

I've included nine tests — on class, place, friends, ethnicity, beliefs, money, career, politics, and life goals — that look at important social and economic factors in relationships, including issues to do with your background, current situation, and future. Why are these socio-economic issues so important? For one thing, issues like career plans and class have a lot to do with one's attitudes and values. They reveal a great deal about your personality and that of your partner, albeit in a slightly less direct way than the tests in the previous section. As with those tests and many of the others in this book, the key element here is similarity. If your politics and aspirations, for instance, are similar then it follows that you are more likely to share personality traits in common.

Looking to the future

The social and economic factors covered in these tests also help to predict what sort of a team you and your partner are likely to make, even after the initial passion that brought you together has faded, including how you are likely to cope with future events such as financial problems or starting a family. In the long run, it is issues like these that determine whether a relationship lasts.

It's a Question of Class

In the 19th century, "class" carried a host of associations and real consequences for people's lives, forming a rigid set of rules that governed the way society worked. People were expected to "know their place," and those who paired up with someone above or beneath their "station" risked social exclusion or worse. Fortunately, today class barriers are much less rigid and it makes more sense to talk in terms of socio-economic status. This is determined by income, education, and aspirations, rather than simply by birth. In general terms, socio-economic status is a very good indicator of whether or not two people are likely to be compatible. This does not mean people in general are obsessed with class, or are even aware of class issues when sizing up a partner. It certainly does not mean that class prejudices of any sort are a good idea, or that you should only look for a partner within "your class." It simply means that comparing your socio-economic category with your partner's helps add another piece to the mosaic of factors influencing compatibility.

Experts such as marketing executives have developed sophisticated schemes for categorizing socio-economic groups, but my test simply distinguishes between three broad categories. No value judgments are attached to any of the categories. You need to complete the test once for yourself and again for your partner.

The Questionnaire

1 Which income bracket do you fall into?

a Low.
b Medium.
c High.

2 Did you go to a private school?

a Yes.
b No.

3 What level of education did you receive?

a High school.
b College.
c Post-graduate.

4 Did either of your parents go to college?

a Neither.
b One.
c Both.

5 Which of the following type of newspapers do you read mostly?

a None.
b Tabloids.
c Broadsheets.

6 Which of the following best categorizes the sort of vacation you normally take?

a Luxury hotels / cruise.
b Foreign package tour.
c Independent / exploring / adventure / activity break.
d Rented cabin.

7 Do you own your own home?

a No.
b Yes.

8 If you had / have children of your own, would you want them to leave education earlier if it meant that they could go straight into a high-earning potential career, or go on to graduate school and take their chance on another opportunity?

a Yes, would want them to start working.
b Would want them to go on to graduate school.

9 During your late teenage / early adult years, how much financial help did you receive from your parents?

a None / very little.
b A fair amount — e.g. helped with college expenses.
c A lot — e.g. bought home / trust fund.

INTERPRETING THE RESULTS

Work out your scores according to this table:

Question/Answer	a	b	c	d
1	6	3	1	-
2	0	6	-	-
3	6	4	3	-
4	3	2	1	-
5	4	4	2	-
6	2	0	6	2
7	4	2	-	-
8	5	2	-	-
9	6	2	0	-

A score of 31–52 places you in category A. You didn't have much growing up, and probably neither did your parents before you. You sometimes struggle to make ends meet.

A score of 19–30 places you in category B. You are most likely to be conscientious and hardworking, and are well aware of the value of money. Life is not necessarily financially easy but you get by.

A score of 12–18 places you in category C. You are most likely to have been used to the flow of wealth in your family and may take this for granted. Provided you also are a high earner, this is fine, but if you are not, you may find life a struggle.

Scores that place you and your partner in the same category indicate a high compatibility rating in this area.

Scores that place one of you in category A and the other in category C indicate a low compatibility rating.

Scores only one category apart indicate an intermediate compatibility rating.

Although comparable socio-economic status is an indicator of compatibility, it's a fairly minor one, particularly for the vast majority of couples who are in the same category or only one apart. A big difference in socio-economic background, however, can be a significant relationship stumbling block and is something that you and your partner should take seriously as it is likely to affect your respective values, aspirations, and expectations. If they differ, conflict is much more likely, and, crucially, it will be harder to negotiate future problems because you may lack the common ground to fully understand one another.

WHAT TO DO ABOUT A MISMATCH

If you and your partner are in opposite categories, the likelihood is that you are well aware of the issues this raises, and may have already talked about them at length. This is fine when you are discussing things in a calm, reasonable way, but the danger times are when emotions run high or things are stressful. This is when you revert to your old, ingrained patterns of behavior and the shutters come down, preventing you from appreciating your partner's perspective. Be prepared by identifying and dealing with likely flashpoints ahead of time. When you do get into tense situations, follow these three simple rules for avoiding class-based antagonism:

- Don't take cheap shots (e.g. "you were born with a silver spoon in your mouth").
- Count to ten before responding; don't rise to the bait if your partner pushes your buttons. By pausing for a second you can regain a bit of perspective and avoid making a bad situation worse with a knee-jerk response.
- Don't jump to easy conclusions. OK, you may have differing socio-economic backgrounds, but don't assume that these are the root cause of an argument. Explore other reasons that are also an issue.

Surprisingly, in this mobile age, most people still find their life partners within their local area, although the definition of local has expanded considerably with time. Your neighborhood, in the sense of the area in which you grew up, is something that you may well take for granted. But, as a significant aspect of your childhood, your neighborhood was a big influence on your formative years. Different communities and environments foster different personal styles. Growing up in the countryside, for instance, might have meant that you were able to roam at will and became independent and self-reliant during your childhood, but bored and restless in your adolescence. Growing up in an impersonal urban landscape might have given you a nervous disposition, or meant you had to develop a tough shell and weren't properly able to express your needs and insecurities.

If these analyses seem clichéd, think about your own experience, and you'll start to see just how significant an influence your environment was. It probably determined which school you went to, who your friends were, what sort of leisure activities or hobbies you did (or couldn't do), what your idea of a good night out is, and what sort of neighbor-hood you favor as an adult.

A childhood/adolescent environment can be equally significant through its impermanence and/or instability. People who moved about a lot as children will probably be only too aware of the issues that result. A typical example is that of "army brats" – people whose parents were in the military and found themselves moving from base to base. Army brats whom I have counseled often express feelings of rootlessness. They cite feeling like outsiders with a subsequent longing for community, or they have experienced difficulty finding a settled life. The upshot of this is that sharing similar childhood environments is a major indicator of likely compatibility – you have, literally, common ground. The distance between your place of birth/upbringing and that of your partner is a way of measuring this tendency toward emotional similarity. Although it is not a precise science, you can discover much that is thought-provoking.

The Test

1 Find a map of large enough scale to show both your "neighborhood" and your partner's, and measure the straight-line distance between them with a ruler. Pay careful attention to the scale on the map and use this to convert your measurement into miles. The most difficult part of this test can be deciding where your "neighborhood" is. Where you "come from" is purely subjective. For the majority of people it's a fairly simple matter, but for some, it's hard to decide between the city, a district, or a region. If in doubt, use the place where you received most of your education.

2 On your map, or one of a larger scale, measure the distance between the two biggest cities in your country. Use the scale to convert this into miles. If you come from different countries, use the distance between countries.

3 Now divide the first figure by the second one to get your "relative origin distance" (ROD). This gives you a result that takes into account the geographical size of your country and the population density.

INTERPRETING THE RESULTS

ROD of 0.5 or less You and your partner are highly compatible in geographical terms.

ROD of 0.5–1 Intermediate geographical compatibility.

ROD of more than 1 Low geographical compatibility.

You need to use a bit of common sense to filter your results, because cultural distance can be much greater than physical distance. On one hand, a distance of 1000 miles might separate two small towns in the Midwest, but the inhabitants might share a huge amount of common ground. On the other hand, some parts of France and England are just 30 miles apart, but the cultural gulf between the two can be total.

WHAT TO DO ABOUT A MISMATCH

Mismatching geographic backgrounds can be a source of conflict because of the way they color your world view and give you differing sets of coping skills. Obviously, you can't change your area of origin, but this is another good example of a test that can help improve your compatibility by stimulating thinking. Consider what your geographical backgrounds have in common as well as what makes them different. A useful exercise is to make a list under the headings "In Common" and "Different."

For example, if you can't see why your partner finds Saturday shopping in the mall so stressful, stop and consider that he/she might not be as comfortable in crowds as you are. Or if your partner doesn't understand why you've got itchy feet after a week lazing on the beach, explain that you're used to a bit more activity and your restlessness isn't a criticism of your relationship.

The Friendship Test

You can't choose your family, but you can choose your friends, so arguably they reveal as much about you as the family history we looked at in the last section. Here we look first at your friendship patterns and then at what you really think of each other's friends.

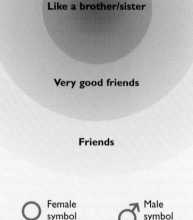

Like a brother/sister

Very good friends

Friends

♀ Female symbol   ♂ Male symbol

Test 1: Friendship Patterns

Are you the sort of person who has just a few very close friends, or do you have a wide circle of acquaintances? Use the Friendship Wheel to compare your friendship pattern with your partner's.

HOW TO USE THE FRIENDSHIP WHEEL

Try to think of all your friends. For each friend, place a symbol on the layer that most corresponds to how close you are to that person. Use male symbols for male friends and female symbols for female friends. Now use your wheel to answer the following questions and compare your answers with your partner's:

- **How many friends do you have in total?**
A big mismatch could indicate that one of you is more introverted and less sociable than the other. More friends means more demands on time, which could cause conflict over how much time to spend together.

- **How many of your friends fall into the central zone?**
These are the people who, in some senses, compete with your partner for your attention and affection. A mismatch suggests that you look to your friends to fulfill differing needs. Those with many very close friends may be looking for a sort of family substitute; people without any look to their family or partner to supply all the intimacy and affection they need.

- **What is the ratio of same sex to opposite sex among your friends?**
A mismatch here suggests that you and your partner have differing approaches to gender relations (the "can men and women just be friends?" question). The obvious consequences of this can be mistrust and suspicion.

- **How many members of your family did you put in the central zone?**
A mismatch here suggests that you have different attitudes about your family. One of you is much closer to sisters, brothers, cousins, etc. than the other, who in turn may not feel so comfortable spending a lot of time with "in-laws."

Test 2: What Do You Think of Your Partner's Friends?

Below are a few common social scenarios. Use your experience of being with your partner's friends in such situations to answer the questions – if you haven't experienced the exact scenario, think of one similar, or use what you know of them to imagine the scenario.

1 You're at a dinner party with your partner and his/her friends. The conversation turns to politics and personal attitudes toward it. Which of the following best characterizes the responses of your partner's friends?

a *Pretentious.*
b *Dull.*
c *Interesting.*
d *Bigoted.*

2 You're at a cocktail bar with your partner and his/her friends. It's late in the evening, a lot of alcohol has been consumed and the music's getting louder. Which of the following best describes how your partner's friends behave?

a *They have good fun.*
b *They are over-the-top.*
c *They are boring.*
d *They behave inappropriately.*

3 An old friend of your partner's (of the opposite sex) is out for the evening with the two of you. How does he/she act toward your partner?

a *Flirtatious.*
b *Possessive.*
c *Supportive.*
d *Reserved.*

4 You're at dinner with a bunch of your partner's friends and their partners. You soon find that the party has sorted into same-sex cliques – your group starts talking about drugs. What goes through your mind?

a *How boring – they're all so old before their time.*
b *How boring – they're all so silly and immature.*
c *It might be an interesting conversation if any of them could stop talking about themselves for one second.*
d *At least a few of them are on my wavelength.*

INTERPRETING THE RESULTS

Score 1 point for the following answers only: 1 c; 2 a; 3 c; 4 d. How did you score? If you got 2 or less it sounds like you don't think much of your partner's pals.

WHAT TO DO ABOUT A MISMATCH

OK, so you don't get along with your partner's friends – don't panic. Focus on the friends with whom you do get along and look to develop your own social life as an alternative so that you don't feel left out if he/she is out without you. Even better, work on developing new social outlets jointly, so that you can make new friends as a couple. Be careful, however, about trying to "reform" your partner's choice of friends or making ultimatums along the "it's them or me" line.

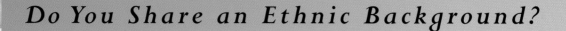

Do You Share an Ethnic Background?

Although ethnicity is a factor, it is, thankfully, much less important for couples nowadays than it has been historically. It's still the case, however, that a shared ethnic background is a powerful influence on compatibility.

Most western societies have attempted to become multicultural over the last few decades, but it is easy to overestimate the number of mixed marriages: most people still partner up with someone of the same ethnic group. From a social point of view, this may not be such a good thing, as insular ethnic communities can lead to a range of social problems, but in relationship terms it fits well with the Rule of Similarity, which states that similar ethnic backgrounds mean you and your partner are more likely to share similar social and cultural values, ethics, aspirations, aesthetics, family dynamics, and attitudes to money.

The Questionnaire

The simplest and most obvious form of ethnicity test is to describe your ethnic background and see if it matches your partner's, but your description will probably take short-cuts and doesn't take account of the fact that some people actively embrace their partner's ethnicity, even when they don't share it. The questionnaire below offers a more complex approach.

1 Do you and your partner relate to your parents in similar ways?

a *Yes – we both love and respect our parents but feel they should let us run our own lives.*

b *Yes – we both feel duty to parents comes first and foremost.*

c *No – we disagree on how much influence our parents should exert on us now that we are adults.*

2 How do you and your partner feel about the type of food your families cook?

a *You both enjoy a wide range of culinary styles.*

b *You distrust food that isn't the way you used to get it at home.*

c *One of you can't stand the other's family cooking.*

3 Do you or your partner use a foreign language or slang that comes from your ethnic background (e.g. Spanish, Yiddish, Hindi), particularly when talking to family members?

a *No, or Yes – but you don't make a big deal out of it.*

b *Yes – one or both of you do and the other is making an effort to learn it.*

c *One of you does and the other doesn't, and the latter doesn't like it / feels excluded.*

4 How do you and your partner feel about your extended families?

a *Get along with them all right when you see them occasionally.*

b *See them a lot and get very involved in their lives, and vice versa.*

c *Disagree over how much of a part they should play in your lives.*

5 How do you, as a couple, feel your children ought to be brought up, should you decide to have any? If it was a central part of your ethnic background, would you have them circumcised/baptized/confirmed/etc.?

a *Both feel that children should be brought up in an open-minded way that does not privilege one culture over another; so no, would not follow such traditions.*

b *Both feel it's important for children to be brought up in at least one cultural tradition.*

c *Disagree on whether children should be brought up within a cultural tradition or over which tradition to follow.*

6 **How has your partner's family reacted to you, and vice versa?**

a   *Both sets of families have been polite and friendly.*

b   *Your family has received your partner to their collective bosom, and vice versa.*

c   *One or both sets of families have been reserved or even hostile.*

7 **How do you and your partner feel about cultural traditions (for example, family meals, religious ceremonies, etc.)?**

a   *They are interesting and entertaining when they apply, but they're not a big part of your lives.*

b   *They are very important and help to define your identities, both independently and as a couple.*

c   *One of you feels much stronger than the other.*

8 **To what extent should ethnic groups assimilate into mainstream society?**

a   *Both agree that mainstream culture should be dominant and that minorities should assimilate to a fair degree.*

b   *Both agree that ethnic groups are at severe risk of losing their individual identities and should work hard to avoid this.*

c   *Disagree on what a reasonable degree of assimilation is.*

9 **Do you and your partner agree on issues of equality within marriage (or partnership)?**

a   *Yes – both agree that spouses / partners should have equal roles and responsibilities, at least in principle.*

b   *Yes – agree that family life should be divided into spheres of responsibility.*

c   *No – differ on respective roles and responsibilities.*

INTERPRETING THE RESULTS

Mostly As You and your partner are ethnically compatible – neither of you has strong feelings about ethnicity. Where there are diversities, you are happy to be different from your partner.
Mostly Bs You and your partner are ethnically compatible – you both embrace a shared ethnic background. Even if you didn't share the background to begin with, one of you has gone to great lengths to adopt the other's cultural traditions.
Mostly Cs You and your partner may well be ethnically incompatible – you find each other's ethnicity or lack of it to be a bit of a stumbling block. Perhaps you feel alienated, or disagree on principle with your partner's views on tradition.

WHAT TO DO ABOUT A MISMATCH

Ethnic incompatibility can be a serious barrier to a long-term relationship because it involves so many other aspects of life and, in particular, family. Having to choose between partner and parents, for instance, can put an intolerable strain on the most balanced individual. Bear in mind, also, that many people who distanced themselves from their ethnic heritage in their youth often find that they want to re-embrace it as they get older.

Here are some strategies to use to avoid antagonism:

• Spell out areas of disagreement and tackle them when you are both calm – don't let them become ammunition during an argument, when hurtful things might be said.

• Don't let disagreement on ethnic issues become cover for unrelated issues. Many people don't get on with their in-laws. If this is the case for you, don't let it become part of some wider debate about race and culture when it doesn't belong there.

• Agree to disagree on some issues. Not every ethnic issue is a "deal-breaker." If your partner doesn't like chicken soup the way your grandma made it, don't let it ruin your relationship.

• The serious issues are things like whether to convert and how to bring up your kids. Raise these as soon as your relationship is sufficiently serious, because you need to settle them. Once you have reached an agreement, abide by it.

Do You Have the Same Beliefs?

Research into compatibility shows that one of the most important influences on compatibility is matching belief systems. Your religious and spiritual beliefs are central not just to your personality but also to your outlook on life and your system of moral values. Beliefs are one of the big issues on which people find it hard to compromise, so of course it makes sense that they're so important in determining who makes a suitable partner. Perhaps the easiest way of "checking" that your belief systems are compatible is to compare religions, and statistics show that a lot of people do just this – the majority of marriages happen between people who share religious background and/or outlook. In practice, however, people of different faiths (and I include agnostics, atheists, humanists, etc. in this term) may find that they have a great deal in common in spiritual and moral terms. That's why this test asks you about your religious and spiritual convictions in general, rather than questions about a specific religion.

The Test

Rate each statement according to how strongly you agree or disagree with it, using the following scale:

1 Disagree strongly
2 Disagree
3 Neither agree nor disagree
4 Agree
5 Agree strongly

(Where a statement uses the word "God," read divine force or higher power if you follow a non-mainstream belief system.)

1 I believe in God.

I	2	3	4	5

2 I think that religion causes a great deal of harm in the world.

I	2	3	4	5

3 I believe in miracles.

I	2	3	4	5

4 I believe in the Bible/Koran/Other book of law.

I	2	3	4	5

5 I believe that religion is mainly superstition and mumbo jumbo.

I	2	3	4	5

6 I believe that God created the Universe.

I	2	3	4	5

7 I believe that God watches over us.

I	2	3	4	5

8 I believe that moral values are ultimately determined by God or some other higher power.

I	2	3	4	5

9 I believe that moral values are determined by society.

I	2	3	4	5

10 I believe that there is a purpose to all things.

I	2	3	4	5

11 I believe that we are not alone in the Universe.

I	2	3	4	5

12 I believe in some form of fate, karma, or kismet.

I	2	3	4	5

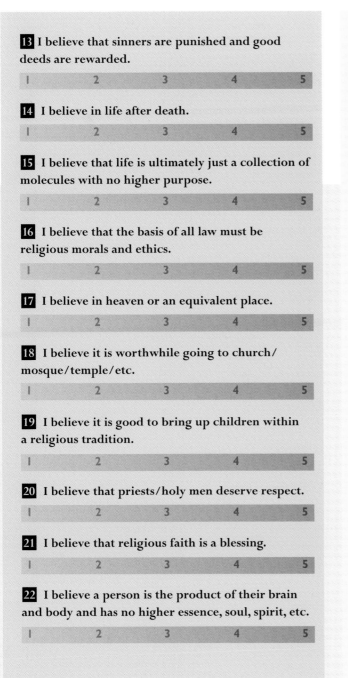

13 I believe that sinners are punished and good deeds are rewarded.

| I | 2 | 3 | 4 | 5 |

14 I believe in life after death.

| I | 2 | 3 | 4 | 5 |

15 I believe that life is ultimately just a collection of molecules with no higher purpose.

| I | 2 | 3 | 4 | 5 |

16 I believe that the basis of all law must be religious morals and ethics.

| I | 2 | 3 | 4 | 5 |

17 I believe in heaven or an equivalent place.

| I | 2 | 3 | 4 | 5 |

18 I believe it is worthwhile going to church/mosque/temple/etc.

| I | 2 | 3 | 4 | 5 |

19 I believe it is good to bring up children within a religious tradition.

| I | 2 | 3 | 4 | 5 |

20 I believe that priests/holy men deserve respect.

| I | 2 | 3 | 4 | 5 |

21 I believe that religious faith is a blessing.

| I | 2 | 3 | 4 | 5 |

22 I believe a person is the product of their brain and body and has no higher essence, soul, spirit, etc.

| I | 2 | 3 | 4 | 5 |

INTERPRETING THE RESULTS

Add up your scores with the exception of those for statements 2, 5, 9, 15, and 22. This sum is your first total. Before adding together statements 2, 5, 9, 15, and 22, subtract 6 from each individual score. Then add these amended scores together. This sum is your second total. Then add both totals together to get a grand total (max possible score: 110). This represents your belief/faith rating. Now compare your rating with your partner's and find the difference. This is your compatibility rating on the belief/faith dimension.

0–30 Highly compatible on the basis of beliefs. You and your partner share similar belief systems so you should be able to avoid major metaphysical disagreements.
30–60 Intermediate compatibility. You might have differing religious convictions or disagree over the details of your respective faiths but you share a common moral compass. Try to keep this in mind if arguments flare over matters of belief or religion.
60+ Low belief system compatibility. There may be an attraction on the base physical level but when it comes to a higher plane you're flying in opposite directions – you may even be on a collision course!

WHAT TO DO ABOUT A MISMATCH

This is a tricky one because religious, spiritual, and moral convictions are not something you necessarily can or should compromise over. On the other hand the questions we've just looked at aren't ones that normally come up in day-to-day life, so you have to balance the practical with the principled. Above all, on such an important issue, you need to look deeper than a test like this will allow. Make time to discuss these issues with your partner in depth so that you know just how far apart you really are.

Money may not be the root of all evil, but when it comes to relationships, it's right up there as the number one cause of strife. A recent survey showed that more than a third of all couples cite money as the principal source of arguments. It was way ahead of children, work, or in-laws. Moreover, a significant proportion of people in relationships hold secret stashes of cash to spend mainly on themselves. For one in ten, this hidden money is actually held "in case of divorce or a breakup." Many would not even tell their partners if they received an unexpected windfall. Yes, money is one of the least romantic topics imaginable. In the first flush of love your assessment of long-term relationship prospects can be

Test 1: Actual Earnings

This test looks at the discrepancy between your salaries. All you have to do is divide the bigger salary by the smaller one. This will give you a number higher than 1, which is the ratio of your earnings.

If one of you is a homemaker, here's how you calculate. If your attitude as a couple is that all money earned by either one of you makes up a joint income and is shared equally, then your salary ratio is 1. Alternatively, if you are not salaried, you can cost your work in the home, and thereby say what your earnings would be if you were paid a salary, using this figure to work out your ratio.

INTERPRETING THE RESULTS

Salary ratio 1–1.5 Evenly matched
Salary ratio 1.5–2.25 Slight discrepancy
Salary ratio 2.25+ Big discrepancy

The more evenly matched your incomes, the less fuel there is for potential disagreements about money, or spending. The bigger the discrepancy in your incomes, the higher the likelihood that conflicting attitudes to money may cause disagreements. In other words, the higher the ratio between your salaries, the lower your compatibility rating will be.

Test 2: Attitudes to Money

Answer the questions and work out your score according to the guide opposite, and get your partner to do the same. Then interpret the results based on the difference between your scores.

1 You see an item of clothing that you like, but you know there are a lot of bills coming in this month and therefore cash might be tight. Do you:
a   *Buy it! It's only money, and you deserve a treat.*
b   *Buy it but feel guilty and tell your partner shamefully if at all.*
c   *Put off buying it.*

2 What do you think is more important?
a   *Being generous and not worrying about money.*
b   *Being generous about big things but sensible about day-to-day expenses.*
c   *Being generous when you can afford to be.*

3 You're meeting friends for a quick drink, but they suggest going for an expensive meal. You know your partner is worried about money. Do you:
a   *Agree – you can't let down friends just to save a bit of cash.*
b   *Steer your friends toward a slightly less expensive venue.*
c   *Make your excuses and stick to the quick drink only.*

4 What's your attitude toward savings?
a   *I don't earn enough yet to start worrying about savings.*
b   *I try to save and usually manage to save something each month.*
c   *I save a regular amount each month, have a pension plan, etc.*

clouded by emotion and also by notions of propriety – it feels inappropriate to have an eye on the bottom line. But once the early stage of romance wears off and the realities of a long-term partnership make themselves known, you will find that money matters just as much to you as a couple as it did to you as an individual.

5 If you earned much more than your partner would you think:

a *I have to spend more on my partner.*

b *I have to make sure my partner gets a fair share.*

c *I deserve to have more say in how our money is spent.*

6 You recently bought a giant-size pack of cereal, but when you got it home the bag inside was open and the cereal was stale. Would you:

a *Throw it out and consider shopping somewhere else next time.*

b *Say you will take it back and get a refund but probably get tired of it hanging around the kitchen and throw it away.*

c *Keep hold of the packet until your next monthly visit to the store and then get a refund.*

7 If you both had salaries but your partner earned much more than you and a big bill arrived for something communal, would you think:

a *My partner paid for the last (smaller) bill; I'll settle this one.*

b *We should split the bill in half.*

c *We should split the bill proportionate to our salaries.*

8 Your partner complains that your high-quality stereo system is getting old. You agree that it looks a bit worn, but it still sounds fine. Do you:

a *Get a brand new high-quality system.*

b *Buy a new – but not as good – one.*

c *Resist replacing a perfectly good system.*

INTERPRETING THE RESULTS

Score 6 for each a, 4 for each b, and 2 for each c. Now calculate the difference between your scores – this is your money compatibility rating.

0–10 You and your partner are highly compatible in terms of your attitude toward money. This might mean that both of you are either extremely careful or extremely wasteful, but at least you see eye to eye. If financial problems arise at least you'll agree on how to handle them.

11-20 You and your partner have some differences over money. Maybe you agree on the major aspects of money management, but not on the details.

21-32 Your attitudes to money do not match and this could cause serious compatibility problems. One partner probably thinks the other is mean – rarely an attractive quality – while the other partner probably thinks the first is irresponsible and possibly selfish – also unattractive qualities, and ones that can cause real anxiety when money matters are involved.

WHAT TO DO ABOUT A MISMATCH

It's very important for partners to talk about money and financial matters because they can so easily have serious consequences outside the emotional realm as well as within it. Nearly half the couples in the survey mentioned earlier disapproved of the way their partners handled cash.

A significant minority (13%) withheld information about the full extent of their annual income. It is easy to grow distrustful in the financial zone because the hurtful disputes can be precisely measured in dollars and cents. If your partner "wastes your money," that can be put down in the account book of life as a number. Many couples find it hard to discuss money because they worry about sounding mean, mercenary, or unromantic. This is why it's a particularly good idea to follow the Rules of Constructive Discussion (see pages 154–5), because these provide a framework for talking about sensitive issues without taking them too personally.

The Career Test

Your career is vitally important to your relationship. It determines how much money you are likely to have, what sort of lifestyle you expect, and what sort of timetable you will follow. Even more importantly, it determines your priorities with regard to your lifestyle. Will you be a beach bum or a banker? If your career is important to you as an individual, think how much more it's going to mean to your long-term relationship!

Couples often get together relatively early in life, before their careers have taken off. This means that although career development is one of the biggest sources of change in a relationship, it's also one of the hardest potentials to assess at the early stages of your relationship. It is for this reason that the following short questionnaire assesses your plans and goals, as well as your current career status.

The Questionnaire

For each question, make one choice for yourself and one for your partner. Score the quiz by comparing your answer and your partner's answer for each question. If they match, score one point. If they don't, score nothing.

1 Have you decided or do you know what career area you would like to pursue?
Yes.   *No.*

2 Where are you in your career?
- *Haven't started/just starting out.*
- *Established.*

3 Is your career/preferred career more about working for others or working for yourself?
Others.   *Self.*

4 Your career/would-be career is creatively fulfilling.
Mostly agree.   *Mostly disagree.*

5 You're at a particularly sensitive time in your career that requires 4 months of working overtime or at weekends, but halfway through this period your partner complains that he/she isn't seeing enough of you. What would you do?
- *Explain that there's only two more months of this to go through.*
- *Try to scale back your working hours even though your career might suffer.*

6 In terms of your career, it is important to you to make a lot of money.
Mostly agree.   *Mostly disagree.*

7 It is important to you to get to the top of your career.
Mostly agree.   *Mostly disagree.*

8 It is important to you to achieve recognition in your field.
Mostly agree.   *Mostly disagree.*

9 You are focused and persistent in achieving your career goals.
Mostly agree.   *Mostly disagree.*

10 Which of these is more important in your career?
Security.   *Fulfilment.*

11 If your job meant moving abroad for a significant period, would you agree to do so?
Yes.   *No.*

12 Do you have a career timetable in mind?
Yes.   *No.*

13 You think at least one partner should put his/her career on hold when you have kids.
Mostly agree.   *Mostly disagree.*

14 Looking ahead, when do you think you might want to retire?
Sooner.   *Later.*

INTERPRETING THE RESULTS

Add up your scores and check them against the following:

0–5 You have a high degree of incompatibility on the career front. This is serious! You and your partner are going in different directions, and the mismatch between your priorities is going to get worse. You have differing values and goals – fundamental differences that could be hard to reconcile. You need to do some soul-searching before you commit to one another in the long-term.

6–10 You and your partner have some differences to overcome before you can be assured that you are both going the same way with regard to important life decisions/plans. But if you focus on the similarities, you can see that you share some important attitudes and aspirations. This is an example of an area where some complementarity can be a good thing and might even improve your long-term compatibility. Some of the most successful couples are those where one partner fits the traditional model of a businessman/woman and the other follows a more creative path.

11–14 Highly compatible. You and your partner agree on many of the "big things" in life and share similar values, goals, and priorities. The only danger arises if you are both at one extreme of the career spectrum – both driven career-obsessives or both directionless slackers – you may not be able to temper one another's excesses, but you may not mind anyway.

WHAT TO DO ABOUT A MISMATCH

Major incompatibilities cannot easily be resolved, but they can be overcome. To make things work, you will need to be sensitive and tolerant with each other, maintaining this care throughout your relationship. Obviously, you must talk over important issues, negotiate, and reach compromises, but to do this productively you need to establish ground rules. The Rules of Constructive Discussion (see pages 154–5) will help, but here are some other helpful guidelines:

• There is no right or wrong approach to having a career, and your way isn't better or worse than your partner's.

• Topics such as these can't be resolved in a single discussion or overnight. Agree to start a process of talking about these issues.

• Try to recast your differences as complementary to each other(see pages 8–9).

Research by an internet dating agency reveals that one of the seven most important compatibility criteria for women is politics; specifically, that their partners' political views match their own. The same result does not apply to men; they are much less likely to be bothered if they vote differently from their partners. Nonetheless, if it's an important issue for one half of the couple, then it's an important issue for the couple as a whole.

The Questionnaire

The simplest way to compare your political views is obviously to see which party you would vote for if there was an election tomorrow, but interpreting the result depends on the political landscape in your country. The US, for instance, is mainly a two-party state, which limits your options in giving an answer and isn't necessarily very informative anyway – the two parties themselves are quite close on a number of issues while the spectrum of opinion represented under each umbrella is considerable. Similar problems apply in many other countries.

A more useful test is one that assesses your views on a range of political issues in order to place you along the liberal-conservative spectrum. Compare your score on this test to your partner's, and use the difference to ascertain your compatibility rating on this topic.

1 To whom does tax collected by the government belong?
a *You and the other taxpayers.*
b *The government and the nation.*

2 Do you support the use of affirmative action?
a *Yes.*
b *No.*

3 Do you believe that minority groups are adequately represented at the highest levels of government?
a *Yes.*
b *No.*

4 Do you think that World War III hasn't happened because of or despite the massive build up in nuclear weapons that's taken place since WWII?
a *Despite.*
b *Because of.*

5 Are people born in this country entitled to more rights than those who emigrate here as adults?
a *Yes.*
b *No.*

6 Do you support a woman's right to choose (abortion)?
a *Yes.*
b *No.*

7 Do you favor the death penalty in cases of extreme crimes?
a *Yes.*
b *No.*

8 Which is the greater injustice: a guilty man acquitted or an innocent man convicted?
a *The former.*
b *The latter.*

9 Would you mind if your child married someone of another ethnic group/religion/culture?

a   *Yes.*

b   *No.*

10 Do you believe the correct response to social breakdown is:

a   *Tougher laws.*

b   *Higher spending on social programs.*

11 Do you believe that it is right to use lethal force against people who break into your house?

a   *Yes.*

b   *No.*

12 Do politicians take enough account of the will of the majority?

a   *Yes.*

b   *No.*

13 Have your political views changed much in the course of your life?

a   *Yes.*

b   *No.*

14 Which type of political leader do you value more?

a   *One who governs by consensus (i.e. by reaching a compromise between the opposing views of subordinates).*

b   *One who listens to others' views but makes his/her own decisions and then imposes them on subordinates.*

INTERPRETING THE RESULTS

Use this key to see which answer gets a point. Then find the difference between your score and your partner's. The higher your individual score the further to the right you are on the liberal-conservative spectrum. However, the point of the test is to look at the difference between your scores, which tells you how politically compatible you are with your partner.

1 a	4 b	7 a	10 a	13 b
2 b	5 a	8 a	11 a	14 b
3 a	6 b	9 a	12 b	

Difference less than 4 You are highly compatible.

5–9 You have intermediate compatibility.

10–14 You are politically incompatible.

WHAT TO DO ABOUT A MISMATCH

If you and your partner differed by ten points or more then the female partner in particular could be left with severe doubts about the relationship. The male approach to political incompatibility is to argue that political views have little practical impact on your day-to-day life together, but this isn't always true. Opposing views on abortion, for instance, could be devastating should you or your partner ever become pregnant by accident. And although there's much to be said for tolerating each other's differences the "surely we can just agree to disagree" approach can occasionally have some serious problems. A partner who holds such a view needs to be very careful because, if their other half does not, there is a risk of dismissing the need for debate. Refusing to even listen to your partner's anxieties will only reinforce his/her negative reaction.

Do You Share Long-term Life Plans?

All of the issues examined in the six previous tests come together to determine your hopes and dreams for the future; hopes and dreams that are articulated in your life plan – what you hope to do in your life; and your life timetable – when you hope to be doing it. Comparing your life plan with your partner's is a crucial step in deciding whether to commit to a relationship.

Step one of this test is to think about your own life plan and its timetable in the following seven areas:

- Children – Do you want any? If so how many and when?
- Family – Will you want or need to be close to your parents or other family members in years to come?
- Career – The Career Test looked at your attitudes and priorities, but what about your actual career plans?
- Home – Where do you want to live in the long run, and what sort of home do you hope to have?
- Travel – Where do you hope to go? Have you got plans for major traveling?
- Health – What is your assessment of your future health and fitness?
- Leisure – Outside of your career, what else are you committed to and what might that mean in concrete terms at different stages in your life?

Under each of these headings, think about your life timetable five, ten, twenty, forty, and sixty years into the future. Now you're ready to answer the questionnaire and work out a life timetable compatibility score.

The Questionnaire

You and your partner both need to answer the quiz.

1 **When do you want to start having children?**
a *Less than 5 years from now.*
b *5–10 years from now.*
c *10–20 years from now.*
d *Never.*

2 **If your partner's parent(s) became ill, and had trouble running their household unaided, what would you be willing to do (assuming you had enough money)?**
a *Have them live with you.*
b *Live near them (one or both of you moving home, if necessary) so you could help out.*
c *Place them in a nursing home near enough to visit regularly.*
d *Nothing.*

3 **When do you and your partner hope to be well enough established in your careers to feel financially secure?**
a *0–10 years from now.*
b *10–20 years from now.*
c *20–30 years from now.*
d *Probably never.*

4 **Which period of your career do you expect to be the most intense, requiring the longest hours and most attention?**
a *That period is in the past/the next 5–10 years.*
b *The period 10–20 years from now.*
c *The period 20–35 years from now.*
d *You'll only scale down your involvement in work when you're too old to carry on.*

5 **Assuming you and your partner don't already own a home together, when do you hope to buy one?**
a *Within 5 years.*
b *5–10 years from now.*
c *10–20 years from now.*
d *More than 20 years from now/never.*

6 **Where would you like to settle in the long run?**
a *In the same town (city/village) where you currently live?*
b *In a different town but the same area (e.g. moving out of the city to the suburbs).*
c *In a different part of the country.*
d *In a different country.*

7 **In what sort of neighborhood/area would you like to settle in the long run?**
a *The city.*
b *Small town.*
c *Countryside/coast community.*
d *Isolated/wilderness area.*

116

8 What sort of travel plans do you have in the future?

a   *Hope to take vacations when you can afford it.*

b   *Hope to spend regular periods of time away (e.g. at second home) when you can afford it.*

c   *Hope to spend a serious period of time (at least 3 months) abroad at some point in the next few years, possibly through your work but not necessarily.*

d   *Plan to go traveling / backpacking for a year or more in the near future.*

9 What sort of health steps would you like to take over the next two decades?

a   *Give up smoking and most drinking; follow a health-food only diet; exercise at least three times a week.*

b   *Cut down on smoking; cut down drinking; eat healthily as much as possible; try to exercise regularly.*

c   *Cut down on smoking; watch your weight.*

d   *None.*

10 Over the next 20 years, how much of your leisure time do you expect to commit to hobbies, sports, or other interests outside the spheres of family and career?

a   *Less than 20 per cent.*

b   *20–40 per cent.*

c   *40–70 per cent.*

d   *More than 70 per cent.*

INTERPRETING THE RESULTS

For each question you get a score based on the closeness of your answers. If you both choose the same letter, score no points. If you are one letter apart (e.g. you: "b"; your partner: "c"), score 5 points, unless one of the answers was "d," in which case score 10. If you are two letters apart (e.g. you: "a;" your partner: "c"), score 10 points, unless one of the answers was "d," in which case score 20. If you are three letters apart (i.e. one of you has chosen "a" and the other "d"), score 30.

0–75 You are compatible.

80–150 You may have problems.

155–300 You have severe compatibility issues.

Since some of the issues covered in this questionnaire are potentially serious, you and your partner should probably exchange answers so that you can talk about important mismatches.

WHAT TO DO ABOUT A MISMATCH

When it comes to major issues that will affect the course of both your lives, such as whether or not to have children or which country to live in, I would advise three basic steps:

• **Discuss the problem early** – If you're going to reach any sort of agreements or compromises, you need to tackle the issues early, before you've invested years in a relationship that may not meet your fundamental needs. However, discretion is needed to judge when a relationship is serious enough to raise such issues without scaring your partner away.

• **Decide deal-breakers** – At some point you may have to decide which you value more – your relationship or your life plan. You and your partner need to think hard about which elements of the life plan are deal-breakers – things you simply cannot do without. The issue of kids, for example, may be non-negotiable, whereas moving to another city might not be such a big deal after all.

• **No regrets/review** – Don't fall into the trap of agreeing to something now in the hope that things may change later, and don't make agreements unless you are very sure you can keep to them. A useful strategy is to agree on a reasonable review period – say, three years down the line – when you can both reflect on your choices and whether you are still happy with them.

PART FIVE

Are You Psychically Compatible?

The use of mystical systems as personality and relationship assessment tools dates back to the mists of prehistory. Take "hedge magic," for example. "Hedge magic" is the kind of folk magic that derives from nature. Even today the first and most common form of "hedge magic" that most of us learn is the "S/he loves me, s/he loves me not" petal test. Such folklore is an example of divination – the use of a paranormal or supernatural system to gain knowledge about the future. Another common form of relationship divination is to peel a fruit in one strip and then drop the peel to get the initial of your destined true love (the odds in this game of love are heavily weighted in favor of people with the initial "S"). Young girls around the world could probably supply a dozen similar tricks.

Stuff and nonsense?

Ardent rationalists would say that there is no such thing as "divine" guidance, but even as a confirmed skeptic, I can see that psychic tests of compatibility have some value. The divinatory systems and theories underlying psychic tests are often complex, and the resulting information can be rich and varied enough for the user to read what he/she wants into them. This means that the tests really can show up something about you as an individual.

This is essentially why things like astrology and palm reading are able to maintain their popularity. But ultimately, the only person who can really judge whether your partner is the one for you is you. If psychic tests provide a way for you to bring to the surface information and opinions that aren't immediately accessible to your conscious mind, then they are providing a useful service regardless of their external validity.

Just a bit of fun?

While psychic testing may not have the scientific basis of the other tests in this book, they are a bit of harmless fun for those who take an interest in magical systems, and they have been used for centuries. They also have real value – they might help you gain a little more insight into your own motivations and needs, and into judgments and assessments about your partner that unconscious parts of your mind have already made – judgments and assessments that could turn out to be surprisingly accurate.

What's in this section?

There are two types of test here. Most of the tests use intuitive systems to try and offer a bit of divination, but two – Do You Believe in ESP? and Have You Had Paranormal Experiences? – look at your beliefs and experiences about the paranormal and the supernatural. Your beliefs and experiences reflect your personality, so in a way these tests are both psychological and psychic.

Beware of the Barnum Effect

Whatever the skeptics say, many people find that their own personal experience of astrology, Tarot reading, palm-reading, graphology etc., shows that these systems can describe their personalities with amazing accuracy. Psychologists, however, have discovered a good explanation for this, and it's got nothing to do with the paranormal. It's called the Barnum Effect, after the legendary American showman, and says that "people tend to accept vague and general personality descriptions as uniquely applicable to themselves without realizing that the same description could be applied to just about anyone" (Robert Todd Carroll, *The Skeptic's Dictionary*). This effect can also apply to relationship compatibility assessments. If a psychic test gives you advice such as "your relationship has had some rocky patches but its positive aspects outweigh its negative ones," be wary – it's not really telling you anything much.

It's in the Stars

Astrology is based on the principle "As above, so below," which holds that things and events in the heavens are somehow linked to things and events on earth. In the case of astrology, the position and movement of heavenly bodies links to human personality and fate.

Recently discovered rock and bone carvings show that at least some of the constellations we recognize today were also recognized by prehistoric humans, but it's impossible to know whether they associated these patterns with human destiny. We do know that astrology was formally codified 5000 years ago by the most ancient civilizations on Earth – those which arose in present-day Iraq and ancient Babylon. Astrological precepts then spread to South and East Asia, where they were modified into different types of astrology. Western astrology is based on the Babylonian tradition.

SUN SIGNS

According to this tradition, the most important aspect of the heavens is the Zodiac – the slice of the night sky inhabited by the sun as it moves around the horizon during the year. Depending on the date you were born, the sun at that time of year would have been rising in a particular "house" of the Zodiac, characterized by one of the zodiacal constellations. The name of the constellation that occupies the part of the sky in which the sun was rising when you were born gives the name of your star sign, or, as it is more properly known, your sun sign. Although astrologers also want to know your ascendant – the sign that was rising on the eastern horizon when you were born – we'll stick with the relatively simple sun sign for this test.

The Test

Astrologers categorize the 12 sun signs according to their relation to the four elements, and the basic rule of sun sign compatibility is that Fire and Air signs are compatible and that Water and Earth signs are compatible (see page 124 for characteristics associated with each element). So the first thing to do is see which of the two groupings you and your partner belong to.

Fire Aries, Leo, Sagittarius	**Water** Cancer, Scorpio, Pisces
Air Libra, Aquarius, Gemini	**Earth** Capricorn, Taurus, Virgo

In practice, the compatibility rules are a little more strict. Consult the table opposite to find out which are the most and least compatible sun signs for your sign.

	Astrological Signs	Most Compatible Signs	Least Compatible Signs
♈	**Aries** March 21–April 20	Gemini, Leo, Aquarius, Sagittarius	Taurus, Virgo, Scorpio, Pisces
♉	**Taurus** April 21–May 21	Cancer, Virgo, Capricorn, Pisces	Aries, Gemini, Libra, Sagittarius
♊	**Gemini** May 22–June 21	Aries, Leo, Libra, Aquarius	Taurus, Cancer, Scorpio, Capricorn
♋	**Cancer** June 22–July 23	Taurus, Virgo, Scorpio, Pisces	Gemini, Leo, Sagittarius, Aquarius
♌	**Leo** July 24–August 23	Aries, Gemini, Libra, Sagittarius	Cancer, Virgo, Capricorn, Pisces
♍	**Virgo** August 24–September 23	Taurus, Cancer, Scorpio, Capricorn	Aries, Leo, Libra, Aquarius
♎	**Libra** September 24–October 23	Gemini, Leo, Aquarius, Sagittarius	Taurus, Virgo, Scorpio, Pisces
♏	**Scorpio** October 24–November 22	Cancer, Virgo, Capricorn, Pisces	Aries, Gemini, Libra, Sagittarius
♐	**Sagittarius** November 23–December 21	Aries, Leo, Libra, Aquarius	Taurus, Cancer, Scorpio, Capricorn
♑	**Capricorn** December 22–January 20	Taurus, Virgo, Scorpio, Pisces	Gemini, Leo, Sagittarius, Aquarius
♒	**Aquarius** January 21–February 19	Aries, Gemini, Libra, Sagittarius	Cancer, Virgo, Capricorn, Pisces
♓	**Pisces** February 20–March 20	Taurus, Cancer, Scorpio, Capricorn	Aries, Leo, Libra, Aquarius

INTERPRETING THE RESULTS

Even within the frame of reference of astrology, this test is a crude approximation of the complex calculations that go into a full horoscope, and astrologers specifically say that their recommendations are guidelines only – the stars may exert a gentle influence, but they do not govern your fate irrevocably.

WHAT TO DO ABOUT A MISMATCH

Don't take a mismatch too seriously. Astronomically-savvy skeptics might point out that because the geography of the night sky changes over the centuries, the sun now moves through 13 constellations on its annual travels not 12. Logically speaking, there should now be 13 sun signs, but few astrologers have risen to this challenge. Perhaps your partner actually belongs to that mysterious thirteenth sign.

For well over 1500 years, Western civilization used a system of medicine that had been set down by the Greeks and Romans. It was based on theories about the makeup of the cosmos and the nature of man that might sound a bit odd to most of us today, but until the 16th and 17th centuries were taken as the gospel truth by learned men and the general public alike. Central to these theories was the ancient Greek notion that the world and everything in it was made up of four basic elements: fire, earth, water, and air. Other civilizations had similar views about the elements, but said that there were more and/or different elements. In Chinese medicine there are five: fire, air, water, metal, and wood; while Indian Ayurvedic medicine also says there are five but names them fire, air, earth, water, and ether.

ELEMENTS AND HUMORS

In the Western tradition, each element gave rise to one of four basic components of the body, known as humors. Humors were thought of as essential fluids that moved around the body causing various physiological and psychological processes. All four humors were thought to be present in everyone, but in different amounts. A preponderance of one of the four was responsible for causing one of four basic personality types, or temperaments.

Table 1 shows the correspondences between the four elements, the four humors, and the four temperaments. Tables of correspondences such as this form the basis of many systems of complementary and alternative medicine still used today, including herbalism, homeopathy, and acupuncture. In fact, correspondences between the elements and other aspects of nature and human psychology extend much farther than this. By the 17th century, alchemists, herbalists, and astrologers had classified practically everything in the world according to correspondence with one of the four elements.

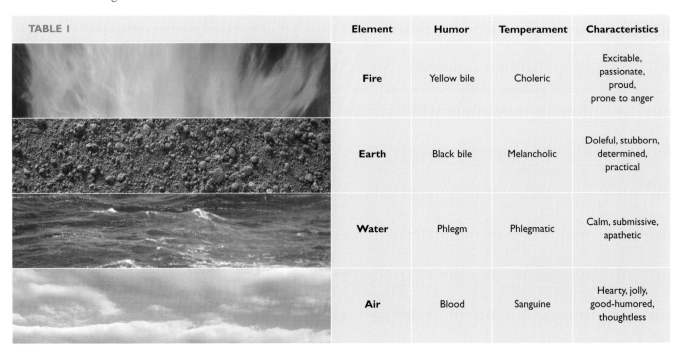

TABLE I		Element	Humor	Temperament	Characteristics
		Fire	Yellow bile	Choleric	Excitable, passionate, proud, prone to anger
		Earth	Black bile	Melancholic	Doleful, stubborn, determined, practical
		Water	Phlegm	Phlegmatic	Calm, submissive, apathetic
		Air	Blood	Sanguine	Hearty, jolly, good-humored, thoughtless

The Test

First you have to work out which categories you and your partner fall into. Table 2 gives some of the many correspondences for the four elements. Use it as a checklist and mark boxes that you feel describe you – the column with the most marks tells you which element, and therefore which temperament, you correspond to most.

TABLE 2	Fire	Earth	Water	Air
Favorite color	Red	Green and brown	Blue	Yellow
Favorite instrument	Guitar and other stringed instruments	Drums and other percussion instruments	Cymbal, bell and other resonant metal instruments	Flute and other wind instruments
Favorite season	Summer	Winter	Autumn	Spring
Favorite time of day	Noon	Midnight	Sunset	Dawn
Strengths	Flexible, creative, passionate	Practical, skilled, determined	Caring, imaginative, expressive	Logical, aesthetic, fair-minded
Weaknesses	Proud, selfish, restless	Stubborn, possessive, unimaginative	Moody, unrealistic, apathetic, submissive	Thoughtless, judgmental, critical
Descriptive phrases	Dramatic, theatrical, hot-blooded, burning with desire	Rooted in tradition, down-to-earth, both feet on the ground, good with hands	Goes with the flow, laid-back, dreamer	Breezes through, head-in-the-clouds, intellectual
Astrological sign	Aries, Leo, Sagittarius	Taurus, Virgo, Capricorn	Cancer, Scorpio, Pisces	Gemini, Libra, Aquarius

INTERPRETING THE RESULTS

Since the four elements relate to one another in specific ways, with some being opposites and some being naturally compatible, by extension, the four humors and the temperaments associated with them assort into mismatched (M in the chart below), compatible (C), and highly compatible (CC). Use Table 3 to determine your compatibility.

TABLE 3				
	Partner 2			
Partner 1	Fire	Earth	Water	Air
Fire	M	C	M	CC
Earth	C	M	C	M
Water	M	C	M	C
Air	CC	M	C	M

WHAT TO DO ABOUT A MISMATCH

There's no need to despair if you and your partner are mismatched in this area. Where this test can be useful is in focusing your attention on aspects of your and your partner's characters that might clash, possibly warning you of future problem areas.

The forerunner of the modern deck of playing cards, the Tarot is a deck of 78 cards with a long and mysterious history. The first recorded appearance is in 14th-century Italy, but they probably draw on much older symbolism – usually dated back to the ancient Egyptians, although there is little hard evidence for this. Originally, only the 22 picture cards known as the Major Arcana were used, but in the late 14th century 56 cards of the type common in Asia, which use 4 suits and have kings, queens, jacks, etc, were added (it's these cards, known as the Minor Arcana, that correspond to our modern playing cards). Although the Tarot was used for card games it is now much better known as a tool for divination.

THE MAJOR ARCANA

Whatever you feel about the "magical" properties of the Tarot, there's no doubt that there's a lot of interesting history and symbolism behind them, especially the Major Arcana, which we'll concentrate on. Anyone who has seen a deck of Tarot cards knows that the Major Arcana do seem to strike a chord. Partly this is down to the layers of mystery they have accrued, but it also reflects their long history as important symbols in western civilization. According to Carl Jung, the Major Arcana represent archetypal figures. In Jung's theory, archetypes are symbols so old and primal that they are embedded not only in our individual unconscious minds, but in a collective unconscious shared by all of mankind. So when we use the Tarot we are using symbols that resonate and maybe even interact somehow with our deep subconscious minds.

Jung's theory is an interesting one but there's no known mechanism by which it might work, unless you believe in the paranormal. But that doesn't mean that a sort of watered down version might not be true. The Major Arcana might not be linked to any higher powers, but they are meaningful symbols and therefore can be used to draw out reactions and feelings from the subconscious. In this case they can be used to help you think about your relationship.

The Relationship Cards

THE FOOL
Both innocent and careless, the Fool can also be dangerous to himself and others. He doesn't know or recognize boundaries or limits and may get hurt or hurt others. He is also a joker and trickster. This card also relates to setting out on a journey.

THE MAGICIAN
Clever and skilled, controlling and manipulative, the Magician can teach, guide, and inform, but can also dazzle and deceive. This card relates to communication, ideas, and intellect.

THE HIGH PRIESTESS
The High Priestess represents the unconscious – spiritual knowledge, often partly hidden. She can represent deception as well as truth.

THE EMPRESS

The direct Tarot equivalent to Jung's idea of the *anima*, the Empress represents the female side of the psyche, including mothers, homemaking, motherhood, and nature. She is maternal, giving, comforting, nurturing but also can be commanding, domineering, devouring, and terrifying.

THE LOVERS

The Lovers obviously represent love, romance, passion, and sex, and related issues such as couplehood, companionship, intimacy, and commitment. They also can relate to self-absorption, narcissism, and vanity; and to vulnerability and the loss of innocence.

THE EMPEROR

The Emperor represents the *animus*, the male principle. He represents authority, control, justice, fairness, and protection, but also can be authoritarian, dominant, inflexible, hard, and uncaring.

THE HERMIT

A guru figure representing wisdom, age, and authority, the Hermit also can relate to isolation and withdrawal. He symbolizes spiritual and physical renewal by contemplation, followed by the application of newfound wisdom to existing problems. This card can signify that answers will come from within.

THE HIGH PRIEST OR HIEROPHANT

Representing spiritual and psychological piety, solidity, and dogma, the High Priest is in touch with the spiritual and relates to firmly held beliefs and convictions. However, he also represents stubbornness, and unwillingness to explore the spiritual or emotional, as well as truth.

THE HANGED MAN

An ancient symbol believed to relate to pagan religions, the Hanged Man represents transformation through self-sacrifice; also, the need to approach things from a different angle.

DEATH

Death may look scary but is actually a symbol of change – of the old order being replaced by the new. As such, he is an opportunity for positive things to happen, if you can let go of the past.

THE DEVIL

Symbolizes arrogance, selfishness, and pride, and also self-imposed bonds, the Devil can sometimes be an addiction – physical or emotional. This card can be interpreted positively as a sign of ways to free yourself from the shackles of a relationship.

THE SUN

A positive card, the Sun indicates health, warmth, optimism, happiness, and opportunity. It represents satisfaction, success, and hope for the future.

THE TOWER

This may not be an obvious relationship card, but it symbolizes upheaval. In relationship terms, it can mean a big – even catastrophic – change, with subsequent opportunities for new beginnings. It also can be a warning that you must change your ways.

The Test

Obviously, you'll need a pack of Tarot cards to do this test. For the sake of simplicity, limit your reading to only those cards in the Major Arcana that relate directly to men, women, and relationships (the ones described on these pages), and arrange them so that they are all the same way up.

Shuffle these 13 cards together. To perform one of the simplest forms of Tarot reading, lay five of the cards out in a cross shape.

4

2   1   3

5

1 The central card represents yourself and shows how you feel about the relationship and where you stand in relation to your partner.

2 The card to the left represents the current state of the relationship and highlights any key issues.

3 The card to the right to represents the future – where the relationship is heading.

4 The card at the top represents your conscious attitudes toward the relationship.

5 Finally, the card at the bottom represents your subconscious attitudes toward the relationship.

Bear in mind that there are no real rules here, and that you can devise any arrangement you like and assign any significance you like – they'll all be equally valid (e.g. the top and bottom cards could represent what your family and friends think of your partner).

Use the card definitions to make your own interpretations about your current emotional state; your relationships past and present; your hopes and fears for the future; and your superficial and deep feelings about your partner and your relationship. Ask yourself questions and use your interpretations of the cards to answer them.

INTERPRETING THE CARDS

The skeptical view of divination techniques such as Tarot reading is that they are examples of a psychological phenomenon called apophenia – the tendency to perceive meaningful links between unrelated things. The human mind has an innate tendency to seek out meaning; with Tarot cards, for instance, this tendency is expressed when we interpret the cards as having significance and meaning in relation to the past, present, and future.

For our purposes this apophenia needn't be a bad thing. Instead, use it as a way of drawing out hidden or uncertain feelings and thoughts. The richer the information that you have to interpret, the more able you are to find links and meaning. A Tarot reading provides an extremely rich field of potential interpretations. These interpretations may not be objectively true, but they will be subjectively meaningful – i.e. meaningful for you. In other words, a Tarot reading is at worst a bit of fun, and at best a way to explore your more "hidden" thoughts and feelings.

CARD DESCRIPTIONS

Note on gender: While the figures pictured in the cards may have genders, in practice the cards are unisex and can refer to either gender. What the gender figures refer to are either aspects of your psyche (everyone has both feminine and masculine aspects to their psyche – Jung called these the *anima* and *animus*) or aspects of a situation or emotion. You can take this at face value; a masculine card in your past, for instance, might refer to a man, or to a "masculine" emotion like rage or lust. Or you can interpret it at a more symbolic level; a masculine card linked to a feeling might mean that you were reacting as your father might have. Go with whichever interpretation feels right for you.

The I Ching

A traditional Chinese system of divination, the *I Ching* has been described as "the oldest, most sophisticated and best loved divinatory system in the world." *I Ching* translates as *The Classic of Change*, and refers to the interpretations and commentaries associated with a system of simple pictograms, made up of solid or broken lines. The basic idea is that you pose a question, use coins or some other randomizing device to generate a series of six broken or unbroken lines, which together make up a "hexagram," and read off the possible meanings and commentaries associated with that hexagram from the *I Ching*. You then reflect and meditate on these, and in doing so find guidance.

This system dates back to ancient China and possibly even back into prehistory, when shamans would use bones to spell out the patterns and built up a body of knowledge associated with them. In around 1100 BC this wisdom was written down for the ancient kings of China – according to some enthusiasts, writing evolved in China specifically to record these oracles. Since then the *I Ching* has developed into a quasi-religious system and complete philosophy of life.

YIN AND YANG

The symbols at the heart of the *I Ching* are the pictograms made up of broken or unbroken lines. These lines symbolize two of the basic forces that make up the Chinese cosmology – yin and yang. Yin, represented by the broken line, is the female principle, associated with all things feminine, nurturing, receptive, and maternal. Yang, represented by the unbroken line, is the male principle in nature, associated with all things masculine, dominant, aggressive, etc.

THE TRIGRAMS

Yin or yang lines can combine to form eight possible arrangements of three, known as trigrams. In the *I Ching*, these eight trigrams are said to represent spirits or elemental forces. In a full *I Ching* oracle, the idea is to come up with two of these trigrams, which are then combined to produce a hexagram (a pictogram made up of six lines). The full meaning of an oracle depends on this hexagram, and there are 64 possible hexagrams (because there are 64 possible ways of combining the 8 trigrams). To complicate matters even more, each of the six lines of a hexagram can be what is known as a transforming line, which adds yet another dimension of meaning.

The Test

Even giving a full list of the 64 hexagrams is beyond the scope of this book, let alone giving all the various interpretations and commentaries. Instead, I suggest using the eight trigrams on the following pages and their associated meanings as a starting point for reflection and meditation on your relationship.

First, you need to pose a question. This is not as simple as it sounds. In using the *I Ching* the question is everything, so you are supposed to think long and hard about the exact form of your question, about your identity as the inquirer and about the possible answers you might get and what they might mean to you. Tips include: make the question open-ended rather than simply yes or no; ask questions that feel important to you; ask for general guidance or wisdom rather than specific advice.

LOVE AND THE *I CHING*

The *I Ching* can be used to give advice or a new perspective on any aspect of life, including love and relationships. It can be read at many different levels, from offering straightforward advice to much more cryptic interpretations relating to your philosophy of life or your deep-seated issues. The philosophy of the *I Ching* is that happiness and good fortune come through following the correct path. In relationship terms, this means that a successful partnership depends on following the correct path – being strong at some times and yielding at others; embracing change at some times and persevering at others.

GENERATING THE TRIGRAMS

The traditional method of generating trigrams involves the use of yarrow stalks, but it is extremely complicated and involved. A much simpler method is to flip a coin three times.
If it comes up heads, it signifies a yin, or broken line: ▬▬ ▬▬
If it comes up tails it signifies a yang, or unbroken line: ▬▬▬▬▬
On a piece of paper, write down, one above the other, the three lines (yin or yang) in the order they appeared.
By putting the resulting three lines together, you will arrive at a trigram – e.g.:

This particular trigram is called Chen, or Shake (see page 133).

INTERPRETING THE TRIGRAM

As noted above, the *I Ching* provides interpretations and commentaries, but these are intended mainly as the starting point for further reflection by "turning and rolling the words in your heart," as the *I Ching* instructs the reader. In this extremely abridged version, use the descriptions given below each trigram as the material for your meditations on compatibility and how to achieve it.

THE TRIGRAMS

LI; RADIANCE

Li represents the spirit of fire, heat, and illumination. It symbolizes the power of awareness and things becoming apparent. It is associated with holding things together (graphically it has a central "supple" or yin line that holds together the two strong yang lines). Li is traditionally associated with strange encounters and chance meetings.

SUN; PENETRATING

The Sun trigram represents the spirit of wood and wind and symbolizes maturity, supportiveness, and nourishing power. It is traditionally associated with marriage and new homes, and therefore relates to commitment and new beginnings. Sun is a female symbol that relates to healing hurts and bringing things together.

KUN; FIELD

The Kun trigram, composed entirely of female yin lines, represents the womb and the maternal principle. It symbolizes the power to create, to give form to things, and to bring them out into the open, as well as nourishment, nurturing, providing, yielding, etc. Kun is associated with the Earth and therefore with death as well as life, for the Earth receives the dead.

TUI; OPEN

The Tui trigram represents the spirit of open water, including lakes, ponds, marshes, and the mists that rise up from them. It symbolizes fertilization and enrichment, stimulating conversation, friendliness, and sexual liberality. It is associated with the ability to spread good feelings and convince and persuade. Traditionally Tui is seen as the friendliest and happiest spirit.

CH'IEN; FORCE

This trigram, with its three male yang lines, represents the dragon, a quintessentially male spirit traditionally associated with creativity, strength, and inspiration. Although it can change shape it is always dynamic and forceful. Although dangerous it has the ability to bring great joy.

KAN; GORGE

Kan represents the spirit of rushing water and the gorge carved out by that water (graphically this relates to the fact that it is composed of a central strong line and supple lines on either side). Like rushing water it cannot be stopped but charges on headlong; accordingly it symbolizes taking risks, having courage, focusing energy and overcoming obstacles. It is associated with flirting with danger, risking everything but coming through. Traditionally Kan also symbolizes hidden riches.

8 Have you ever been stuck talking to someone dull at a party and fervently hoped that your partner would come and rescue you, only for him/her to do so? 1 point

9 Have you sometimes been thinking about an obscure movie to watch for a night in, only to have your partner suggest the same one? 1 point

10 Have you ever picked up the phone to discover that your partner was on the other end, calling you, but that the phone hadn't had time to ring? 3 points

11 While spending the night apart, have you ever been awake in the night thinking about your partner, only to discover that he/she was thinking about you at the same time? 2 points

12 Have you and your partner ever shared similar dreams? 3 points

13 When you first met, did you discover that you shared:
A favorite book? 1 point
A favorite song? 1 point
A favorite movie? 1 point
A favorite place? 1 point

INTERPRETING THE RESULTS

0–10 If you do share a psychic bond with your partner there's precious little evidence of it.

10–20 Some strange coincidences have certainly cropped up around your relationship, but then most people could say that.

20+ Strange coincidences abound, but is this evidence for a psychic bond or does it simply show that you and your partner are really on the same wavelength?

HOW SERIOUSLY SHOULD WE TAKE THIS?

The skeptical view is that "evidence" for psychic bonds of the type outlined in this test actually tells us more about how aware a person is of coincidence. According to this theory, coincidences affect almost all of us to roughly the same degree, but some people are much more aware of them, and when they see them are much more likely to interpret them as meaningful. This could be because they are prone to magical thinking or are not so good at judging probabilities, making them more inclined to think that a coincidence is much less likely to be simply the result of chance.

However, even if we accept that coincidences are just that and nothing more, there are factors that can increase their likelihood, such as sharing very similar tastes and habits, being closely attuned to each other's thought processes, and knowing each other well. While these may not constitute a psychic bond, they certainly increase compatibility.

Have You Had Paranormal Experiences?

The final stage in our exploration of paranormal attitudes and experiences is to look at things that have actually happened to you. This test investigates your experiences with the paranormal (beyond the realms of the normal, but supposedly explicable in terms of either existing or as yet undiscovered natural laws) and the supernatural (entirely beyond the realms of the natural universe).

People who have had paranormal or supernatural experiences are often profoundly changed by them. Beliefs and attitudes are especially likely to be altered. This has obvious ramifications for relationship compatibility. A hardheaded rationalist who has never ever had a "weird" experience may find it difficult to relate to someone who's had a profound spiritual or otherworldly experience.

The Questionnaire

This test assesses a number of categories in the world of strange phenomena. In each category there is a series of questions asking about your experiences, starting with fairly innocuous ones and progressing to full-blown bizarre encounters. For each "yes" answer you give, score the number of points shown.

Ghosts

a *Have you felt a cold spot or draft in a house where there shouldn't have been one?* 1 point

b *Have you ever heard footsteps, banging, voices, or moaning from places / rooms that were supposed to be empty?* 1 point

c *Have you ever felt a presence when you knew no one was there?* 2 points

d *Have you ever seen a shape or figure appear out of nowhere, disappear suddenly, or pass through walls / objects?* 3 points

Strange beasts

a *Have you ever seen or thought you saw an animal that looked as if it shouldn't be there?* 1 point

b *Have you ever seen or heard signs of a strange creature (e.g. very large footprints, unearthly howling)?* 1 point

c *Have you ever seen a strange creature, such as Bigfoot?* 3 points

UFOs

a *Have you ever seen a light or form in the sky that did not seem to behave normally (e.g. moving at great speed, changing direction very sharply)?* 1 point

b *Have you seen a flying craft or object of some description that did not resemble anything you've ever seen on Earth?* 2 points

c *Have you ever witnessed a flying craft or object that interacted with you or the environment in some way (e.g. leaving impressions in soil, stopping engines, causing burns or redness)?* 3 points

Alien abduction

a *Have you ever experienced "lost time" — where you suddenly realize that much more time than you thought had elapsed (often while driving), as if it had been lost?* 2 points

b *Have you ever felt a strange presence in your room and pressure on your chest but been unable to move?* 2 points

c *Do you have vague memories of going aboard a strange craft or encountering beings you could not recognize?* 3 points

Psychic experiences

a *Have you ever thought of someone you haven't thought of in ages only to have them phone you out of the blue?* 1 point

b *Have you ever known something specific about someone without being told?* 1 point c *Have you ever performed an uncharacteristic action without really knowing why, only to find it had unexpected consequences (e.g. walking to the store rather than driving, only to discover that there was an accident on the road that day)?* 2 points

d *Have you ever felt or known that something had happened to a partner or other loved one, to discover later that you were right?* 3 points

Religious/spiritual phenomena

a *Have you ever felt guided/protected by a benign presence?* 2 points

b *Have you ever heard voices?* 2 points

c *Have you ever had an out-of-body experience (where you seem to leave your body and float above it, and are able to look back at it)?* 2 points

d *Have you ever seen a vision?* 3 points

e *Have you ever had a near-death experience (where you nearly died and in doing so seemed to have an out-of-body-experience/life flashing before your eyes/seen a tunnel of light)?* 3 points

Other

a *Have you ever lost something only to have it turn up in a place where you had definitely already looked?* 1 point

b *Have you ever seen strange things falling from the sky (e.g. fish, frogs)?* 2 points

c *Have you ever seen a person/scene that seemed to be from another era/place (known as time slip)?* 3 points

INTERPRETING THE RESULTS

Add up your score and get your partner to do the same. Now compare your results. A score below 10 is low, and a score above 25 is high. If one partner scored low and the other high, you have a mismatch.

HOW SERIOUSLY SHOULD WE TAKE THIS?

Skeptics will note that most of the examples of weird phenomena found in this test can be explained in a rational fashion. The alien abduction questions, for instance, cover several commonly reported aspects of the alien abduction phenomena, but most of these could have non-paranormal interpretations. A strange presence in the room together with chest pressure and paralysis are all elements of a phenomenon called sleep paralysis, probably linked to some form of temporal lobe epilepsy. Vague memories of aliens or spacecraft are harder to explain, but since they usually only surface in people who have had hypnotic therapy to "help" them remember, such memories become extremely suspect.

The point of the test, however, is to look at your subjective experience of weird phenomena, whatever the actual explanation. Someone who scores high on this test may actually be psychic or in touch with the supernatural world, or may simply be more prone to magical thinking and have a "fantasy-prone" personality. Such a person is less likely to be compatible with someone who has never had any such experiences.

WHAT TO DO ABOUT A MISMATCH

UFOs, ghosts and monsters may not rate highly on your list of important relationship issues, so you may decide that a mismatch on this test isn't such a big deal. If you do disagree over these issues try not to let your disagreements become personal; don't get sucked into disparaging your partner's views. As always, respect is the key word. You must respect your partner's views, even if they seem odd or closed-minded to you.

This last point is particularly relevant to this field. By their natures, skeptics and "believers" often find it hard to accord each other's views proper respect because to do so may challenge deeply held beliefs, beliefs that become important to personal identity. The solution is to work hard at keeping an open mind while maintaining critical thinking — examine "facts," pose questions, challenge assumptions, avoid emotional reasoning, and consider all of the alternatives.

PART SIX

Putting It All Together

If you've done all the tests in the book you will have worked through over 50 measures of compatibility. On some of those measures you will have come out as highly compatible, while almost certainly you'll have scored a mismatch on others. As you've no doubt realized, some of the tests are more serious than others, and the results you got from them should be taken more seriously. But how can you tell which ones are which, and what sort of overall conclusion should you be drawing from your results?

In this section I'll show you how to get an overall Compatibility Rating (CR) by combining your scores. You don't need to have taken all of the tests – you can get a CR based solely on tests that you have completed.

HOW THE CR WORKS

The aim of the CR system is to convert your scores on each test into a form in which they can be combined, while taking into account the importance of the topic, the provenance of the test and the reliability of the testing method involved. This is achieved by giving each test a weighting factor that reflects these issues.

FILLING IN THE TABLE

There are four steps to working out your overall CR:

1. STANDARDIZE YOUR SCORE FOR EACH TEST

First, you need to convert your score from each test into a standardized form which is then comparable with the scores from other tests. To keep things simple I'm going to limit the possible scoring categories in most cases, so for each test decide whether you were a match, a mismatch, or one of the intermediate categories (where relevant), unless other specific categories were offered (e.g. the Row-ometer Test). Column 2 shows you what score each of these categories corresponds to. Pay close attention to the presence of plus or minus signs.

2. MULTIPLY BY THE WEIGHTING FACTOR

Next, multiply your standardized score by the Weighting Factor (WF) in Column 3. The WF attempts to take into account how serious an impact that topic actually has on compatibility, as well as reflecting the likely validity of the test used to rate it (some tests depend on more makeshift scoring methods than others). You'll notice that some of the WFs are zero – this indicates a test that is "just for fun." Remember to take into account the +/- sign, and also that anything multiplied by zero = zero. Record your standardized score multiplied by your WF in Column 4.

3. TOTAL UP YOUR WEIGHTED SCORES

Total all the weighted scores that you have recorded in Column 4. Don't forget to take account of the +/- signs (e.g. the total of -20 and -20 is -40; the total of -20 and +5 is -15). Column 5 shows sample scores as an example.

4. ADD OR SUBTRACT YOUR TOTAL FROM YOUR BASE COMPATIBILITY RATING

You start with a base CR of 1000. To find your overall CR, simply add or subtract your score (depending on whether it's plus or minus) from your Base CR. What are you left with? (See How Did You Score?, page 151)

Because you start with a base rating, it doesn't matter how many tests you completed and got scores for, your overall rating is still valid and comparable with anyone else's. However, the more tests you do complete, the more accurate your final CR will be.

Test	Standardize your score	Weighting factor	Your score	Example
Middle Finger Test	Match = +100 Mismatch = -100	0.05		-5
2D:4D	Match = +100 Mismatch = -100	0.05		-5
Beauty	Match = +100 Mismatch = -100	0.3		-30
Symmetry	Similar = +100 Not very similar = -50 Totally dissimilar = -100	0.05		-2.5
Smelly T-Shirt	T-shirt rating of higher than 10 = Match = +100 Mismatch = -100	0.05		+5
Energy	Close match = 100 Intermediate = 0 Mismatch = -100	0.8		0
Ideal Profile	Almost identical = 100 Same ballpark = 50 Moderately different = -50 Worlds apart = -100	0.05		+2.5
Age	Match = +100 Mismatch = -100	0.1		+10
Sleep	Close match = +100 Intermediate match = 0 Mismatch = -100	0.8		0
Sexual History	Close match = +100 Intermediate match = 0 Mismatch = -100	1		+100
Adventurousness	Close match = +100 Intermediate match = 0 Mismatch = -100	0.8		+80
Fidelity	Close match = +100 Intermediate match = 0 Mismatch = -100	0.8		-80
Talk	W, X or Y = -100 Z = +100	0.7		-70
Libido	Match = +100 Mismatch = -100	0.4		+40

Your Overall Compatibility Rating

Test	Standardize your score	Weighting factor	Your score	Example
Sexual Style	Very well matched = +150 Match = +100 Depends = 0 Mismatch = -100	0.4		+60
Extroversion	Close match = +100 Intermediate match = 0 Mismatch = -100	1		+100
Conscientiousness	Close match = +100 Intermediate match = 0 Mismatch = -100	1		-100
Openness	Close match = +100 Intermediate match = 0 Mismatch = -100	1		+100
Agreeableness	Match = +100 Mismatch = -100	0.8		-80
Neuroticism	A = +150 B = 0 C = -50 D = -50	0.8		-40
Intelligence	Compatible combinations = +100 Mismatch combinations = -100	1		+100
Emotional Intelligence	Both scored high = +200 Both scored low = 0 Both scored medium = 0 One high, one low = -50 One medium, one low = -100	1		-50
Creativity (Artistic impulses)	TCP difference < 40 = +50 TCP difference 40–70 = -50 TCP difference >70 = -100	1		-50
Creativity (Creative thinking)	Match = +100 Mismatch = -100	0.8		-80
Sense of Humor	Close match = +100 Intermediate match = 0 Mismatch = -100	1		+100
Boredom Threshold	Match = +100 Mismatch = -100	0.8		+80
Happiness	Match = +100 Mismatch = -100	0.6		-60

Test	Standardize your score	Weighting factor	Your score	Example
Life History	Match = +100 Mismatch = -100	0.6		-60
Birth Order	Match = +100 Mismatch = -20	0.6		-12
Family Atmosphere	Close match = +100 Intermediate match = 0 Mismatch = -50	1		0
Likes and Dislikes	Close match = +100 Intermediate match = 0 Mismatch = -100	1		0
Praise: Blame Ratio	P:B > = +150 P:B 2–5 = -50 P:B < 2 = -150	0.8		+120
Arguing style	Green = +150 Red = -100 Blue = -50 Yellow = -100	1		-50
Love	Type 8 = +300 Types 5 and 6 = +100 Type 7 = +50 Types 2–4 = -50 Type 1 = -150	0.5		+25
Class	Close match = +100 Intermediate match = 0 Mismatch = -100	0.5		0
Place	Close match = +100 Intermediate match = 0 Mismatch = -100	0.2		+20
Friends (Friendship Roundel)	Match = +100 Mismatch = -100	0.4		40
Friends (Test 2)	Match = +50 Mismatch = -100	0.6		30
Ethnicity	Match = +100 Mismatch = -50	0.5		-25
Beliefs	Close match = +100 Intermediate match = 0 Mismatch = -100	1		-100
Money (Actual earnings)	Close match = +100 Intermediate match = 0 Mismatch = -100	0.8		+80

Test	Standardize your score	Weighting factor	Your score	Example
Money (Attitudes)	Close match = +100 Intermediate match = 0 Mismatch = -100	1		0
Career	Close match = +100 Intermediate match = 0 Mismatch = -100	1		0
Voting	Close match = +100 Intermediate match = 0 Mismatch = -100	1		-100
Life Plan	Close match = +100 Intermediate match = 0 Mismatch = -100	1		-100
Astrology	n.a.	0		--
Elements and Humors	n.a.	0		--
Tarot	n.a.	0		--
I Ching	n.a.	0		--
Numerology	n.a.	0		--
Graphology	n.a.	0		--
Sheep-Goat	Close match = +100 Intermediate match = 0 Mismatch = -100	0.3		-30
Psychic Bond	Close match = +100 Intermediate match = 0 Mismatch = -100	0.1		+10
Weird-ometer	Match = +100 Mismatch = -100	0.2		+20

INTERPRETING THE RESULTS

As an example, imagine you'd taken all the tests and scored a grand total of −7, which would reflect a pretty fluctuating pattern of results, with plenty of tests where you scored a big fat mismatch, but plenty of others where you and your partner seemed to be in synch. To find your overall CR, simply add, or in this case, subtract (because of the minus sign) 7 from your Base CR of 1000, to get 993. Putting you squarely in the intermediate compatibility range (see below).

HOW DID YOU SCORE?

CR 3000+ You and your partner are made for each other. You have lots in common and share vital personality characteristics, goals, and beliefs. With a little work your relationship could provide you with lasting happiness.

CR 1500–3000 You and your partner are highly compatible but there are plenty of areas where you're not completely in synch. You may have to work hard at times but you have solid foundations on which to build a lasting relationship.

CR 500–1500 You and your partner are intermediately compatible. There are many positives to your relationship and also lots of negatives, but this is true of the vast majority of relationships. Only you will know exactly which areas are letting your compatibility down, and only you can make the judgment as to whether these are deal-breakers or not. If you are willing to work hard and give your relationship the attention it deserves you can have a rewarding long-term partnership.

CR 100–500 You and your partner may not be compatible. Deciding to end a relationship is never easy but you have to consider what's good for you in the long-term.

CR LESS THAN 100 Presumably you sensed that something was rotten in the state of your relationship before you picked up this book. If not, wake up! It looks like you and your partner may be bad news for each other, at least in the long-term. Consider your future together very, very carefully.

The Ancient Romans used to say that nothing human can be made perfect. I don't disagree but surely all of us strive to make the very best secure and loving relationship we can? Between a third and a half of those who embark on marriage, however, come unstuck. The divorce rate for those previously married is even higher. So our ideals need some practical help. At the outset, I assume there is general agreement about the importance of clear communication. Without a problem-solving and explaining system in your family life it is difficult to avoid killer conflict (see the Rules for Constructive Discussion, pages 154–5).

My first suggestion is to treat a relationship as "bigger than you are." Marriage, for instance, is a question not an answer. You cannot control its entire shape, course, and outcome. Be humble enough to accept that sometimes things will go wrong. If you cannot get what you want, can you want what you can get? Or want it a little more than you did at first glance? Try not to run away just because there is disagreement. The grass may be greener on the other side of the hill but it will turn into the same old mud if you keep on voting with your feet.

Second, a relationship that isn't growing is dying. You cannot be in a partnership just because the law says you are. "We got married" is no guarantee of security. Nowadays, few of us need a partner just to survive economically and so a successful relationship depends on the quality of the intimacy between two people. This in turn depends on the qualities of compatibility between two people, and these in turn depend on whether you are prepared to make the effort required to keep the partnership alive.

Third, a first-class relationship needs two people to respond to changing circumstances at roughly the same ratio. The law of life says that change is constant but alas some people pretend they are *not* growing older or can continue to act like children long after they ought to know better. The accusation goes like this: "Your problem is you've changed!" And the reply follows: "And your problem is you haven't!"

Fourth is trying to maintain respect. Quite often, you may hate your partner's behavior. They may have been selfish

YOUR 20-POINT CHECKLIST FOR A PERFECT PARTNERSHIP

1 Being able to say sorry – the next day.

2 Being able to wait for the other person to say sorry – the next day.

3 Having genuine common interests, similar quirks, complementary vices, and virtues.

4 Wanting the other's good opinion.

5 Enjoying mutual silence/time off.

6 Giving permission to say the unpopular or voice anxieties.

7 Giving verbal encouragement always.

8 Reading the other's moods.

9 Taking second place often enough.

10 Being given first place often enough.

11 Learning each other's skills – work/domestic – so each is the other's backup.

12 From day one, sorting out money issues.

13 Making criticism constructive/using assertion skills – "I'd prefer this ... I won't tolerate that."

14 Touching – especially when things are difficult.

15 Planning and having fun.

16 Being open-minded about new ideas or adaptable to change (age/outlook/capacity/habit) at roughly the same rate or ratio.

17 Dragging a problem out by the teeth when necessary to move it on.

18 Respecting the other's family – within reasonable limits.

19 Being forgiving.

20 Learning how to enjoy domestic life – since we all end up in an armchair eventually.

or careless but it is always better to avoid labeling them. Instead of saying "You're useless" specify which of their acts you will no longer tolerate. Instead of writing them off as "failures," give them definite choices. "You can either talk this through with me or I will start to lose my interest in us. Is that what you want? You decide."

Fifth comes respect for personal space. Nobody truly wants to live in someone else's pocket apart from the odd clothes fetishist and those requiring personal therapy. We have a very important relationship to develop with ourselves, as well as with others. Solitude is as good for the soul as socializing. Being joined at the hip, or asking someone "Do I have salt on my potatoes?" is a recipe for a coma. So before you get involved with a grown-up in a relationship be confident that you can lead your own independent life. This will give you enormous strength in the struggles to come.

Sixth is a matter of respecting priorities. If you are in a "primary" relationship the word implies that when the chips are down you will put the other person first. Of course there will be conflicts of interest, for example you would rather be in the restaurant than nursing your partner's influenza or attending the funeral of one of their relatives, but remember that since you are "doing it for the relationship" you are also doing it for yourself.

Finally, realize that what actually matters is your delivery. You can be filled with fine words of love but what you actually "mean" is what you do. If you keep calling someone "sweetheart" but are generally bitter, you do not mean what you say. If you say you love your partner but continue to belittle them or undermine their confidence, it is more likely you dislike or even hate them. Love is *not* really expressed in fantastic acts of financial generosity but in small, consistent daily gestures of affectionate respect. A touch on the cheek; a small passing caress. These alone can "purchase" love; these alone will make it last.

The Rules of Constructive Discussion

The number one rule in relationships is that communication is key. Communication is the lens through which your relationship problems pass. If you have poor communication, your problems will be magnified; if good, they can be minimized. If communication breaks down, you will both be in the dark. There is no way back. A dialogue of the deaf or a sulking stalemate will be your fate. That's why I think it's a good idea to end this book with a quick resumé of the rules of constructive discussion.

If you follow these rules you can discuss practically any issue and reach a compromise/resolution without hurting each other. At the very least you can maintain respect for one another and avoid making a difficult situation worse. Obviously, if the relationship is in meltdown already and there is no goodwill left, it is probably pie in the sky to think you can do all this without professional help. I am assuming here that feelings are not completely out of control. At the start of a relationship, there is more going on than meets the eye. It isn't simply that two people start living together. In effect, two different family systems collide. Differences can include attitudes toward religion, food, tidiness, time-keeping, anger, bad language, even hygiene. "We do things this way – you do things that." In addition, conflict is normal in a healthy relationship. On many occasions, healthy vital human beings will fail to agree about "what to do next." Research into successful relationships reveals that it's not whether you have rows that counts, but how you conduct them. Learning to manage these differences rather than reverting to childhood fury or sulking is much of the battle. The rest is down to improving your communication skills by using the following rules.

THE 12 RULES OF CONSTRUCTIVE DISCUSSION

1 Find time to talk. You should even consider making an "appointment," when you will both put everything else on hold in order to have a proper discussion.

2 Pick the time wisely – don't wait until just before bedtime, or when you are tired, depressed, or hungry.

3 At all costs don't "stonewall" or refuse to have a discussion at all. You may not be able to talk right now because you are too distressed or angry but at the very least agree to talk at a later time. Stonewalling has been shown to be the single most destructive form of behavior in a relationship. It is something men do more than women (though both are guilty at times) because they are strongly averse to criticism which they regard as an overt challenge to their masculinity.

4 Decide in advance how long you are going to spend on your discussion, but also agree that either one of you can take "time outs" as necessary.

5 Practice active listening skills. a) One person goes first and the other listens without interruption. b) Afterward, the listener sums up what the other has said. c) The first speaker agrees that that is what they did say. d) Only then does the second person respond. This helps the listener to take in what is said and minimizes misunderstandings.

6 It may be useful to have a pen or a bunch of keys as a token and agree that "the only person who can speak is the one holding the 'magic' token". Flip a coin to see who goes first. When person "A" has said their piece and been understood, hand the magic token to person "B".

7 State your differences. Make sure you really know what the other person is saying. Give them permission to speak freely "on any topic" but don't feel you necessarily have to reconcile every disagreement. Listening without retaliatory comment is one of the basic techniques of conflict resolution.

8 Use non-judgmental language. Say "I need…" or "I feel…", rather than "You are…" or "You always…" or "You never…". The verb "to be" is the judgment verb and can cause destruction whereas what you "feel" is unique to you. It cannot be challenged and does not hang a label on the other person.

9 Remember that the aim is not to try to win – if you "win" the relationship loses. This highlights a big difference between the worlds of work and home. In business, the idea is to win a contract, sell at a profit, beat the other guy to the job. The essence of capitalism is competition. But if you live by the same values within the family you will destroy your relationship. (If you convincingly "prove" your spouse is incompetent, then it suggests you were incompetent in marrying them!)

10 Having stated your differences, learn that it's okay to accept them. It's perfectly all right to have some degree of difference even on serious issues like politics or religion. Being in a good, close loving relationship does not mean wearing identical opinions.

11 Actively look for a deal or compromise. What will you give to get some of what you need? No one gets everything, so compromise is essential.

12 Try to find the common ground. Remember that this is the first casualty of conflict when we focus on what we lack, what we want, or what we miss. Often it is only after a serious conflict has caused damage that you realize what you are losing in the effort to "gain" something more.

INDEX

ACKNOWLEDGMENTS

The author would like to thank:
My ex-es for teaching me about incompatibility – and my family, friends, and BACP colleagues for the opposite lesson. A special thank you to Joel Levy without whom this book would not have been completed. I also owe much to my clients for sharing privileged information over many years. A big credit must go to Amy Carroll for suggesting the project and to Louise Dixon for expert editing of the text.
Phillip Hodson, London, June 2004.

Carroll and Brown would like to thank:
Illustrators David Newton/*Début* Art and
John McFaul/Central Illustration Agency
Additional design assistance Jim Cheatle
Production Karol Davies
IT Paul Stradling
Proofreader Geoffrey West
Indexer Helen Snaith